AF538278

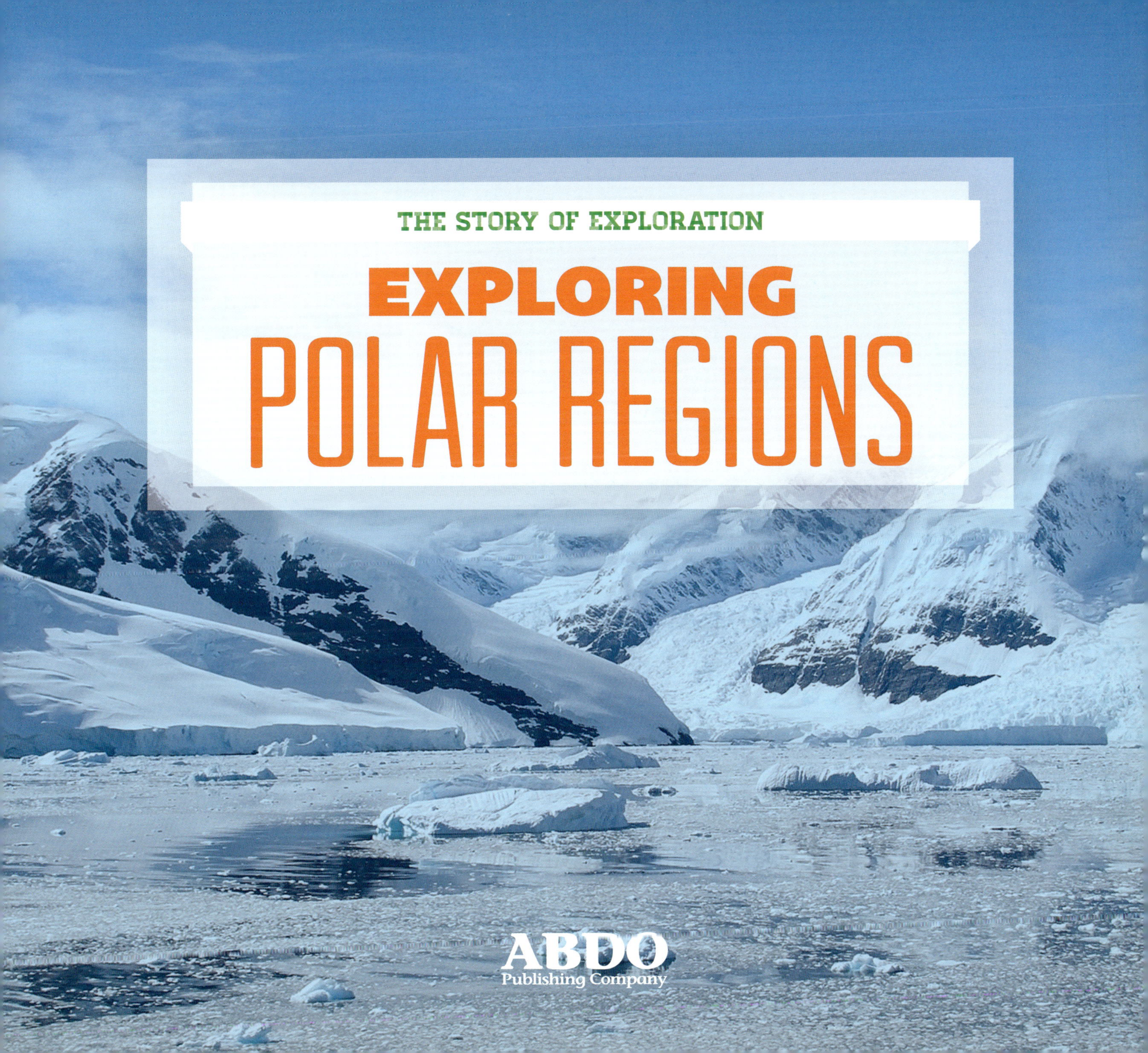

THE STORY OF EXPLORATION

EXPLORING POLAR REGIONS

ABDO
Publishing Company

EXPLORING POLAR REGIONS

BY JUDY DODGE CUMMINGS

CONTENT CONSULTANT
GORDON HAMILTON
ASSOCIATE PROFESSOR, CLIMATE CHANGE INSTITUTE & SCHOOL OF EARTH & CLIMATE SCIENCES
UNIVERSITY OF MAINE

CREDITS

Published by ABDO Publishing Company, PO Box 398166, Minneapolis, MN 55439.

Printed in the United States of America,
North Mankato, Minnesota
102013
012014

 THIS BOOK CONTAINS AT LEAST 10% RECYCLED MATERIALS.

Editor: Arnold Ringstad
Series Designer: Emily Love

Photo credits: Shutterstock Images, cover, 2–3, 47; Dan Bach Kristensen/Shutterstock Images, 6–7; Minden Pictures/ SuperStock, 10–11; George Tyson, 13; Intrepix/Shutterstock Images, 16–17; Vitaly Korovin/Shutterstock Images, 18–19; Library of Congress, 21, 58; Kurt and Rosalia Scholz/SuperStock, 24–25; North Wind Picture Archives, 26–27, 74; Image Asset Management Ltd./SuperStock, 31, 78; Nathaniel Dance-Holland, 35, 133 (top left); Newberry Library/SuperStock, 36–37; I. Pilon/Shutterstock Images, 39; Nils Strindberg, 41; Adam Burton/Robert Harding Picture Library/SuperStock, 42–43; Hendrik Hondius, 44–45; Bettmann/Corbis, 48–49, 54–55, 60, 111, 113; AP Images, 57, 70–71, 86–87, 96–97, 133 (bottom left); George R. Lawrence, 62–63; Harris & Ewing, 65; Corbis, 76, 133 (top right); Henry Bowers, 82–83; Michael Van Woert/NOAA, 85; Agentur Voller Ernst/picture-alliance/dpa/AP Images, 91; US Government, 92; Mike Dunn/NOAA, 98–99; Frank Hurley, 102–103; Cliff1066/Flickr, 106–107; US National Archives, 109, 133 (bottom right); Wolfgang Kaehler/SuperStock, 116–117; Davor Pukljak/Shutterstock Images, 119; Alaska Stock/Alaska Stock-Design Pics/SuperStock, 120; Yva Momatiuk & John Eastcott/Minden Pictures/Corbis, 123; Rex Features/AP Images, 126; Kaspersky ONE Trans-antarctic Expedition/Kaspersky Lab/AP Images, 128–129; Volina/Shutterstock Images, 132; Red Line Editorial, 132

Library of Congress Control Number: 2013946591
Cataloging-in-Publication Data

Cummings, Judy Dodge.
Exploring polar regions / Judy Dodge Cummings.
p. cm. -- (The story of exploration)
Includes bibliographical references and index.
ISBN 978-1-62403-252-3
1. Polar regions--Juvenile literature. 2. Polar region ecology--Juvenile literature. 3. Polar regions--Discovery and exploration--Juvenile literature. I. Title.
910.911--dc23

2013946591

CONTENTS

The Greenland tundra became an important frontier in early Arctic exploration.

CHAPTER 1

MURDER, MAYHEM, AND MUTINY IN THE ARCTIC

Four men trudged across the Greenland tundra toward a rock cairn. When they reached it, they dug into the frozen soil until their shovels hit a coffin. They pried open the lid, revealing a dead body wrapped in an American flag. One man straddled the coffin and sliced open the corpse, examining its organs. The men clipped the corpse's frozen fingernails and snipped some hair from its head. Then, they sawed off the top of the dead man's skull and removed his brain.

These men did not seek to violate the dead. Some suspected the dead man had been murdered, and they sought justice for him. However, for Captain Charles Hall, justice came 96 years too late. His experiences on the *Polaris* expedition showcased the struggles of polar exploration—man versus nature and man versus man.

THE *POLARIS* EXPEDITION

In 1870, Captain Charles Hall prepared to lead the first US expedition to the North Pole. No human had yet reached either the North or South Pole. Explorers from across the globe hungered for the glory such achievements would bring. On the eve of his journey, Hall introduced his crew to the American Geographical Society, a group of professional geographers: "I have chosen . . . men who will stand by me through thick and thin. Though we may be surrounded by . . . icebergs, and though our vessel may be crushed like an eggshell . . . they will stand by me to the last."[1] Hall was wrong.

Tensions between Hall and Emil Bessels, the doctor in charge of scientific research aboard the *Polaris*, began before the ship left port. Hall insisted the primary purpose of the mission was to reach the North Pole. Bessels believed science should dictate where the crew went and how fast they traveled. Hall won the debate, but an unhappy Bessels spread dissatisfaction among the other crew members.

The *Polaris* departed New York City, New York, on June 29, 1871. By August it had reached Greenland, where two Inuit hunters, along with their

LATITUDE AND LONGITUDE

Two great invisible lines divide the Earth. The equator divides the planet into northern and southern hemispheres, and the prime meridian divides it into eastern and western hemispheres. Polar explorers use these lines to calculate locations in latitude and longitude.

Latitude and longitude are measured in degrees, minutes, and seconds. There are 60 minutes in one degree and 60 seconds in one minute. Latitude lines run parallel to the equator and are used to measure distance north or south of the equator. The equator itself sits at 0° latitude, the North Pole is at 90° north, and the South Pole is at 90° south. Longitude lines, also known as meridians, run from the North Pole to the South Pole. The prime meridian, which runs through Greenwich, England, is located at 0° longitude and is used as a reference to measure distance east and west of the line. There are 180 degrees east of this line and 180 degrees west of it. Any location on Earth can be given by providing its latitude and longitude.

families, joined the expedition. Then the *Polaris* traveled north to Smith Sound, a narrow sea passage between Canada and Greenland. The 55-mile (88 km) strait of ice-clogged waters was a treacherous obstacle.[2] The crew member in charge of steering the ship, Sidney Buddington, feared getting stuck in the ice. He wanted to suspend the voyage to wait out the winter, but Hall ordered him to forge ahead. By early September the ship reached 82° north. Surrounded by icy waters, Buddington refused to go farther. Hall relented and the crew prepared to spend the winter on the northern coast of Greenland.

Tensions seethed on board. Buddington constantly criticized Hall and was often drunk. When Hall went on a two-week excursion inland, he left George Tyson, the assistant navigator, in charge. Hall told Tyson he planned to fire Buddington when he returned. When Buddington

Hunks of ice drift throughout the polar seas.

discovered this he told Tyson, "Oh, I'll get out of [trouble]. [Hall] won't live long."[3]

Two weeks later, Hall returned from the excursion healthy and invigorated. That night he drank a cup of coffee and complained it was too sweet. Then Hall turned pale, doubled over with stomach pains, and lost all sensation on his left side.

Bessels diagnosed it as a stroke and treated Hall's fever with quinine. He mixed the white crystals with a liquid and injected the concoction into Hall's leg. Hall became delirious and accused people of poisoning him. He banned Bessels from his bedside, refusing medical treatment.

In early November, Hall seemed to recover and allowed the doctor to treat him once again.

THE ARCTIC ENVIRONMENT

The name Arctic stems from the Greek word *arktikos*, or "northern." An imaginary line called the Arctic Circle surrounds the Earth at 66° 33′ 44″ north. Everything north of the line is considered to be the geographic Arctic. The northernmost parts of Europe, Asia, and North America stretch into the Arctic. The Arctic Ocean fills the remainder. For most of the year, the surface of the Arctic Ocean forms into pack ice averaging 12 feet (3.7 m) thick.[4] Underneath this ice the Arctic Ocean averages less than one mile (1.6 km) deep.[5] There is no permanent land at the North Pole, the northernmost point on Earth. The average temperature at the North Pole is –40 degrees Fahrenheit (–40°C) in the winter and 32 degrees Fahrenheit (0°C) in the summer.[6]

An investigation ruled Hall died of natural causes, but many believed Bessels was responsible for his death.

On November 6, Hall received an injection, ate a big meal, and told his officers he would join them for breakfast the next day. But later that night, Hall's tongue swelled and he struggled to breathe. He died on November 8, 1871. The crew wrapped his body in an American flag and buried him in the frozen arctic soil.

After Hall's death, anarchy ruled the ship. The crew got drunk and played cards late into the night. Buddington handed out loaded revolvers to several men. Eventually, spring arrived. The crew made attempts to reach the pole, but the ice proved to be an impossible barrier. Finally, the *Polaris* headed for home. Before the ship got far, ice seized it again.

The night of October 15, 1872, a gale hit. The ship creaked and moaned under the ice pressure. Leaks sprang in the hull, and Buddington ordered all supplies thrown overboard onto ice floes so they would not go down with the ship in case it sank. Bags of flour, boxes of meat, and tons of coal were tossed over the sides. Much of the valuable food and fuel plunged through the ice and into the ocean depths.

Several crew members, including Tyson, spent the night hunkered down on the ice floe outside the ship. In the middle of the night, the ice broke up and huge chunks began drifting apart. By the time Tyson woke up, he discovered that he, nine other crew members, and the Inuit families were marooned on a piece of ice approximately one mile

(1.6 km) in diameter.[7] All they had with them were a few tools, nine dogs, two small boats, two kayaks, and a small amount of supplies.

The stranded group could see the *Polaris* approximately eight miles (13 km) away.[8] Tyson tried to catch the ship's attention, but the *Polaris* slipped around a bend. The group had been abandoned on a chunk of ice adrift in the Arctic Ocean.

The nightmare began. The group drifted along, battling hunger, waves, and wind. The Inuit built igloos and fashioned tin can lamps fueled by seal blubber for heat and light. But seals were scarce and the Inuit men were the only competent hunters. The group slowly began to starve.

Their Thanksgiving dinner in 1872 was raw, frozen seal guts.

MAGNETIC AND GEOGRAPHIC POLES

The Earth has several different poles. The poles most commonly referred to are the geographic poles at 90° north and 90° south. These poles define the axis of Earth's rotation. However, there are also magnetic and geomagnetic poles. The magnetic North Pole is the location to which magnetic compasses point. It is currently located at approximately 82° north, 113° west, a point in Canada's extreme north. It is slowly moving to the northwest. The geomagnetic North Pole represents one end of the Earth's own magnetic field. It is located at approximately 80° north, 72° west.[9]

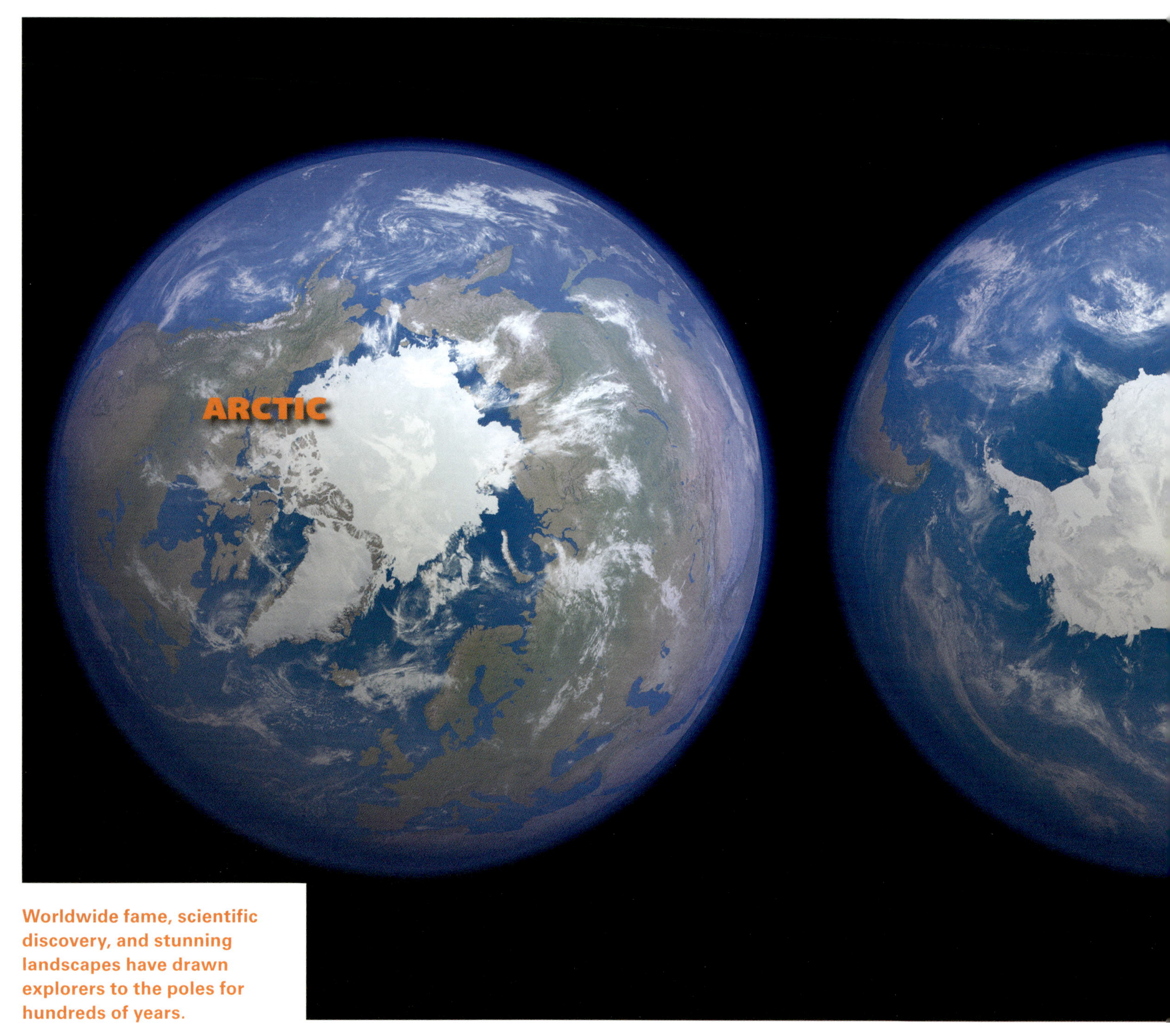

Worldwide fame, scientific discovery, and stunning landscapes have drawn explorers to the poles for hundreds of years.

The Inuit couple with whom Tyson shared an igloo worried some crew members were eyeing their children hungrily. Tyson wrote, "Cannibalism! If it is God's will that we should die by starvation, let us die like men, not like brutes, tearing each other to pieces."[10]

As spring arrived, their ice floe began to melt. On April 1, 1873, the group climbed aboard one of their small boats and began traveling south. They camped upon ice floes. One night, a massive wave swept most of their remaining supplies into the sea. Death drew closer.

On April 30, a whaling ship broke through a fog bank and came upon the stranded men and women. Its crew stared in disbelief at the broken-down heap of humanity that drifted alongside the ship. The 19 people had survived on an ice floe for 197 days, drifting more than 1,500 miles (2,400 km).[11] The rest of the crew of the *Polaris* was also rescued. They had survived the winter in northern Greenland, aided by local Inuit. In spring, they set out in two small boats and were rescued by a Scottish whaling ship.

During the investigation into the death of Captain Hall, Tyson, Bessels, and Buddington were all questioned. However, Hall's journals had disappeared, witnesses' testimonies were conflicting, and Hall's body was far away in Greenland. Investigators concluded Captain Hall died of natural causes.

That was the official record until 1968. In that year, scientists traveled to Greenland and exhumed Hall's body. They discovered it contained arsenic. This poison tastes sweet, perhaps explaining why Hall had complained of overly sweet coffee shortly before his death. Arsenic causes the throat to swell and leads to hallucinations, paralysis, and death. Though the evidence showed Hall had been poisoned, the identity of his murderer remains a mystery.

The windswept desolation of the poles has attracted explorers for centuries.

The *Polaris* expedition demonstrates the extremes to which people have gone in the course of their explorations. Whether they pursue glory, scientific discovery, or simply survival, they fill the history of polar exploration with tales of human character at its best and worst.

THE LURE OF THE ENDS OF THE EARTH

Frostbite. Barren sheets of ice. Never-ending darkness. Few people would willingly risk their lives in the hostile environments of the Arctic or Antarctic. The words of polar explorers themselves reveal the irresistible attraction of the poles.

Some of them show a hunger for adventure. As his ship sat frozen in the Arctic ice pack in 1894, Norwegian explorer Fridtjof Nansen wrote, "I was simply a child yearning for a great adventure out in the unknown . . . the great adventure of the ice, deep and pure as infinity, the silent, starlit polar night."[12]

The desire for fame drew other men to break polar barriers. In 1899, frostbite caused the skin of Robert Peary's

In addition to being a polar explorer, Nansen won the Nobel Peace Prize for his work helping refugees.

heels to cling to the inside of his boots when he pulled them off, but he still refused to leave the Arctic. He desperately wanted to be the first man to reach the North Pole. He once told his mother, "I will be foremost in the highest circles . . . and make powerful friends. . . . Remember, mother, I must have fame."[13]

Scientific curiosity also compels people to the frozen ends of the earth. Richard Byrd was the first man to fly over the South Pole in 1929. This was a dramatic journey for the record books, but Byrd also recognized the importance of his aerial surveys of the Antarctic mountains. "They lay in the shape of a crescent; their spurs and crags rising . . . out of the snow. Here was something to put on the map: a fine new laboratory for geological research."[14]

Other explorers simply love the desolate beauty of the ice. In 1871, Captain Charles Hall said,

THE ANTARCTIC ENVIRONMENT

The name Antarctic comes from the Greek word *Antarktikos*, or "opposite to the north." Unlike the Arctic, Antarctica is a landmass. It sits below the Antarctic Circle, at 66° 33' 44" south. Antarctica is covered by an ice cap nearly three miles (4.5 km) deep in places.[15] The South Pole is marked with a plaque.

Summer temperatures in Antarctica's interior average –18 degrees Fahrenheit (–28°C). In the winter, the average plummets to –76 degrees Fahrenheit (–60°C).[16] Antarctica is extremely dry, receiving an average of less than two inches (5 cm) of precipitation per year. No native people live in Antarctica. Only scientists and Antarctic station crews live on the continent.

"The Arctic region is my home. I love it dearly—its storms, its winds, its glaciers, its icebergs . . . it seems as if I were in an earthly heaven."[17]

Viking settlements in the Arctic, reduced to ruins today, represent some of the earliest European explorations of the area.

CHAPTER 2

QUESTS FOR A NORTHWEST PASSAGE

In approximately 325 BCE, the ancient Greek explorer Pytheas journeyed to the far north. On a ship with oars and a large square sail, Pytheas sailed across the Mediterranean Sea and past what is now the United Kingdom to a land he called Thule. This place was too cold for cattle or crops, summer nights were only two hours long, and Pytheas considered the people "barbarians."[1] Historians disagree on whether Pytheas landed on Norway or Greenland. Regardless of where he actually landed, Pytheas's voyage is among the earliest recorded European trips to the Arctic.

LAND OF BANISHMENT

Murder pushed Europeans back to the Arctic hundreds of years later. The Vikings were a seafaring people from Scandinavia who launched raids against the coastal towns of Europe beginning in the 900s CE. When warriors were accused of murder, they were banished from their homeland. One exiled Viking settled on Iceland and established a colony there in 874. In 965, Erik the Red arrived at the colony after being banished from Norway

IMAGINARY LANDS

When nothing is known about a place, people often fill in the gaps with their imaginations. The Greeks described a race of people called the Hyperboreans who lived at the top of the world. The Romans believed that in the north, snow fell constantly like feathers. European sailors in the 1200s believed in a polar sea with huge whirlpools populated by mermen with icicle-shaped heads. As late as the 1600s, a French traveler said Arctic people were "sorcerers who control the winds at will."[2]

Erik the Red brought settlers to Greenland in the 980s.

for murder. Then he committed murder in Iceland and was banished yet again. With no other options, Erik sailed for a land rumored to lie west of Iceland. He eventually found a frozen island and explored it for three lonely years. When his banishment expired, Erik returned to Iceland with exaggerated tales of a fertile land to the west. Settlements were soon established on what he called Greenland.

The Vikings continued searching for new lands. From Greenland they sailed to Labrador and Baffin Island off the east coast of modern-day Canada. Erik the Red's son Leif Eriksson was the first European to step foot on mainland North America. He spent the winter in a place he called Vinland. Historians believe this was likely the area now called L'Anse aux Meadows in Newfoundland. Leif's brother, Thorvald, encountered Inuit

VIKING SHIPS

Gales and giant waves are common in the North Atlantic. The Vikings mastered these conditions in ocean-going vessels called *knarrs* and dragon-headed longships called *drekars*. They nailed oak planks in an overlapping pattern to construct light, yet sturdy ships. Knarrs could carry up to 24 short tons (22 metric tons). Archaeologists discovered the remains of a longship that was 119 feet (36 m) long, with room for 72 oars and a 100-man crew.[3]

natives, a people the Vikings called Skraelings. One of them shot Thorvald with an arrow. The explorer's last words were: "We have won a fine and fruitful country, but will hardly be allowed to enjoy it."[4] After only a decade, the Vikings left mainland North America. By 1500, experts believe, expanded sea ice cut off trade routes between Greenland and Europe. This may have been what led to the collapse of the Viking settlements.

RACE FOR RICHES

Cinnamon, pepper, and silk beckoned the next wave of explorers to the Arctic. Portugal and Spain controlled the trade routes that snaked around the southern tip of Africa to China and the East Indies. Overland

THE REAL CONQUERERS OF THE ARCTIC

Native people lived in the Arctic for thousands of years before the arrival of Europeans. Historically, most groups were nomadic. Inuit in northern Alaska followed herds of reindeer and caribou. Those in northern Canada and Greenland hunted seals, walrus, and whales. The Arctic Ocean was a major food source, and whale blubber provided fuel. Inuit men fashioned igloos from blocks of snow, and women cured animal skins and sewed parkas for protection from the polar winds. A diet of raw meat rich in vitamin C protected them from scurvy. The native people built sealskin kayaks and trained dog teams to pull their sleds. When European explorers eventually reached this icy world, those who learned from the Inuit had the best chance of survival.

routes existed, but transport was much easier on water. In an age when nutmeg and cloves were worth more than gold, Europeans searched for an alternate ocean route to the luxury goods they craved. The hunt for a northwest passage along the northern coast of North America to Asia became an obsession for European explorers.

The adventures of these explorers reveal the challenges they faced. The Italian John Cabot was hired to explore on behalf of England in 1497. He reached Newfoundland but did not find the Northwest Passage. Cabot attempted to find it again the following year but his fleet never returned to England. No further historical records of Cabot have been found. It is assumed his expedition was lost at sea.

The English launched another expedition in 1576, this time led by Martin Frobisher. He discovered a large bay in what is now known as Nunavut, Canada. The body of water now bears his name. Certain he had found the Northwest Passage, Frobisher sailed into the bay. He encountered Inuit people traveling in sealskin kayaks. Frobisher sent three men to barter with the natives. The emissaries were never

Frobisher would go on to make two more voyages in search of the Northwest Passage.

seen again. In return, Frobisher captured Inuit men and took them back to England. The men drew much curiosity from Europeans, but they soon died. The lives of native people would be forever changed as Europeans continued to explore the north.

The Northwest Passage was discovered during this early era of exploration, but no one realized it at the time. In 1615, William Baffin and Robert Bylot explored Hudson Bay and sailed north through the Davis Strait. They discovered the Smith, Jones, and Lancaster Sounds, the doorways to the passage that can transport a ship from the Atlantic Ocean to the Pacific Ocean—if the ice is open. But Baffin and Bylot did not explore far enough to realize the significance of their discovery.

A NORTHEAST PASSAGE

Explorers also made attempts to find a Northeast Passage. In 1596, the Dutch sent William Barents to attempt to sail east along the northern edge of Europe. By the end of summer, his ship was locked in ice north of Norway. That winter, 17 men crammed themselves into a shelter made of driftwood and ship planks. They survived on bear meat, though some men sickened from toxins in the bear livers. Barents's men repaired two small boats and managed to return home to the Netherlands in 1595. That was the end of Dutch efforts to find a Northeast Passage.

BETWEEN ASIA AND NORTH AMERICA

In the 1300s, Russia established bases around the White Sea in its northwest region to reap profits from fur trapping, a lucrative industry. Then a leader emerged who took an interest in science as well as money—Peter the Great. In 1724, he created what would become the Russian Science Academy and appointed Vitus Bering, a Dane, to lead an expedition to sail east and find where Asia and North America connected.

The expedition set out from Saint Petersburg, Russia, in 1725. The explorers traveled by horse-drawn sled to Okhotsk, a settlement more than 3,400 miles (5,500 km) away on Russia's east coast. They arrived in 1727. There, the crew spent several months making a *shitik*. They used willow twigs and leather strips to sew planks together to create this flat-bottomed boat. The men lived off the land, extracting salt from the sea, using fish oil instead of butter, and distilling liquor from grass. Finally their vessel was finished in July 1728, and they launched into the Sea of Okhotsk and headed north.

Bering sailed for a month, passing 67° north. He entered a narrow channel that separates Asia from America, a body of water now called the Bering Strait. A heavy fog prevented him from spotting the coast of North America. However, on a second Russian expedition in 1734, explorers definitively sighted the American coast and the Aleutian Islands, proving Asia and North America are separate continents. One of the men on the expedition explored the Aleutian Islands by kayak and reported hundreds of sea otters along the shore. His report led to a surge of Russians heading east to trap furs. Soon whale hunters followed. The maps of these hunters added to the world's knowledge of the geography of the Arctic.

The search for the Northwest Passage continued. In 1776, the British directed Captain James Cook to find the route. Cook traveled through the Bering Strait to 70° north until pack ice blocked his way. Cook created the first reliable map of the Bering Strait and the coast of Alaska, but he did not find the Northwest Passage.

THE DOOMED FRANKLIN EXPEDITION

In the early 1800s, the British restarted their exploration of the Arctic. John Franklin, an experienced explorer, begged to lead an expedition to explore the uncharted sections

Cook made key early explorations in the world's northern and southern oceans.

of the Arctic Archipelago. The Royal Navy hesitated. Franklin was 59 years old. A colleague of Franklin's told naval officials, "If you don't let him go, the man will die of disappointment."[5]

John Franklin had been an Arctic explorer for decades. He had previously survived a harrowing expedition to northern Canada in the 1820s.

Franklin set sail in May 1845. Two years passed with no word from the expedition. In the fall of 1848, relief ships were sent to find them. They found nothing. Franklin's wife asked US President Zachary Taylor for help and even sought assistance from a psychic. Rescue parties launched rockets and kites, hoping survivors would spot them. In 1854, the Royal Navy gave up the Franklin expedition for dead.

Later that year, an officer of the Hudson Bay Company, a French fur trading company, reported what he had learned from a group of Inuit. Four years earlier, the natives met 35 white men heading south on ice toward the Boothia Peninsula. Their ship had been crushed in the ice. Later, the Inuit found bodies of white men farther south. From the mutilated corpses and the contents of the camp kettles, the Inuit concluded the Franklin expedition had resorted to cannibalism. The English refused to believe it.

One author called the natives "cruel . . . gross . . . uncivilized people . . . [who live on] blood and blubber."[6]

Lady Franklin dismissed this report and hired another relief ship. Finally, in 1859, searchers found a stone cairn containing two messages from the Franklin crew. The first, dated 1847, said simply, "All well."[7] The second message was dated 1848. It explained the ship had been stuck in the ice since 1846. Franklin and 24 other men were dead. The survivors were heading for the Canadian mainland, 200 miles (320 km) to the south.[8] They never arrived.

Though rescuers never located the lost Franklin expedition, their years of searching resulted in the discovery and charting of previously unknown lands and waterways. The map of the Arctic was almost complete. Only the northernmost areas of the globe were still labeled as being unknown. Explorers cast their sights on the North Pole. In the following decades, they began to set out for the pole in ships, sleds, and even balloons.

The islands and intricate waterways of the Arctic were nearly all mapped by the mid-1800s.

GREENLAND
Arctic Circle
BAFFIN'S BAY
DAVIS STRAIT
HUDSON BAY
HUDSON STR.
LABRADOR
BRITISH
RUPERT
CANADA
Gulf of St Lawrence
Grinnell Land
Ellesmere Id.
North Devon
North Lincoln
Lancaster Sd.
Melville Sound
Banks Land
Pr. Albert Land
Victoria Land
Cockburn Island
Gulf of Boothia
Boothia
King William Land
Wollaston
Mc Clintock Chan.
Cumberland Sound
Frobisher Strait
Fox Land
Fox Channel
Southampton Isd.
James Bay
Iceland
C. Farewell
Mackenzie Bay
Gt. Bear
Athabasca
Wollaston Lake
Deer Lake
Fort Chipewyan
Fort Churchill
Fort Nelson
L. Superior
Ontario
Michigan
Halifax
Quebec
Montreal
St Lawrence
C. Sable
Liverpool
Newfoundland

MISSION IN FOCUS
THE ANDRÉE EXPEDITION

In July 1897, Salomon Andrée and two colleagues set off from Spitsbergen, an island north of the Norwegian mainland. Their destination: the North Pole. Their transportation: a hot air balloon.

Things went wrong from the start. The balloon's basket dipped into the water upon takeoff. Safety latches accidentally released hundreds of pounds of ropes designed to stabilize the airship, sending the balloon hundreds of meters into the sky. Still, Andrée wrote in his diary, "To be the first to have floated here in a balloon. . . .We think we can well face death, having done what we have done."[9] After the balloon drifted out of sight, the explorers were never seen alive again.

In 1930, a Swedish scientific expedition landed on desolate White Island. The scientists discovered a stove, books, a boat lashed to a sled, and human bones. Inside one skeleton's jacket was a diary. Andrée had been found. His detailed diaries and rolls of film tell the story of the men's last days.

Three days after leaving Spitsbergen, the balloon crashed on the ice. The men were 216 miles (350 km) from land and still 480 miles (770 km)

from the North Pole.[10] They began walking. Despite accidents, snow blindness, and severe illness, the men remained scientists. They preserved samples of leaves and clay. They dissected a gull's eyeball. They recorded their diet and their symptoms. The photographs and diaries enabled Andrée to speak from beyond the grave. He recorded details of nature in the Arctic as well the story of the crew's struggle to survive.

Though the continent lay just beyond the horizon, Antarctica remained out of reach of explorers until the 1800s.

CHAPTER 3

IN SEARCH OF A SOUTHERN CONTINENT

The Ancient Greeks believed a large landmass must exist on the southern end of the world to balance the Arctic lands of the north. They called this place Antarktikos. Today it is known as Antarctica. Over the centuries, people fantasized about this mythical land, imagining it to be rich, fertile, and warm.

FIRST SIGHTINGS

The Europeans of the 1500s sought efficient, navigable routes across the oceans to boost their trade revenues. These early explorers provided tantalizing evidence about the mysterious land to the south. Still, many maps of the period included the words *terra incognita*, Latin for "unknown land," over unexplored regions. One of these regions was the theorized yet unconfirmed continent at the South Pole.

Ferdinand Magellan set out westward from Spain on his famous circumnavigation of the globe in 1519. His five ships sailed to Brazil

THE EXPLORER'S SCOURGE

Magellan's expedition ran low on food and survived for a month on a diet of putrid water, biscuits crawling with worms, and ox hide. But even men with sufficient quantities of salt pork and flour fell ill with swollen joints, bleeding gums, and mental instability, and eventually many died. These symptoms were a sign of scurvy, a disease caused by a diet with insufficient vitamin C. Scurvy is fatal but can be easily cured with a diet of fresh vegetables and fruit or raw meat. No one died of scurvy on James Cook's voyages. The diet on his ships included plenty of sauerkraut and marmalade of carrot, foods high in the necessary nutrient.

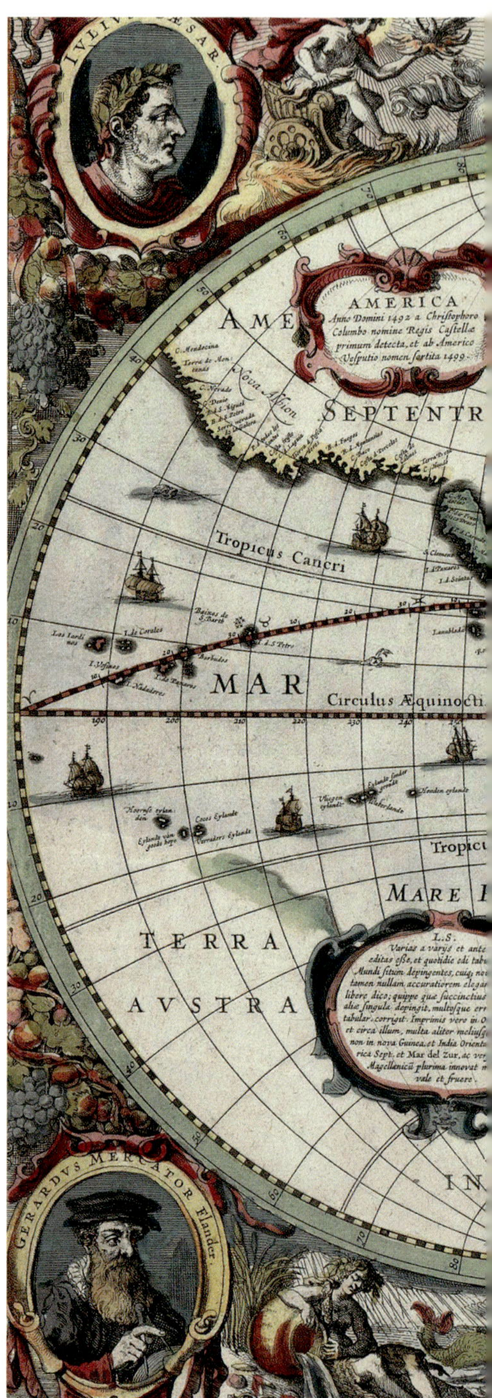

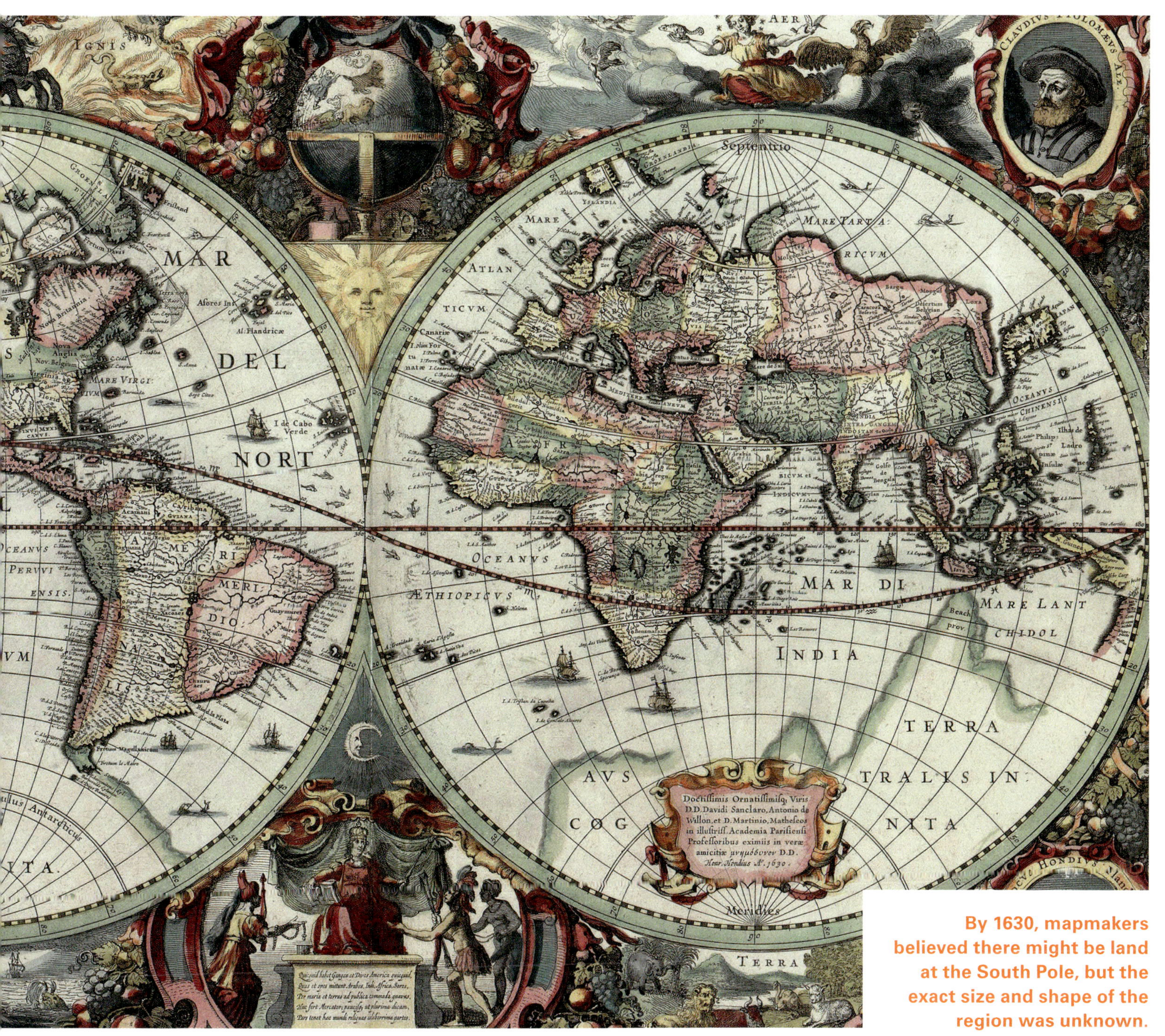

By 1630, mapmakers believed there might be land at the South Pole, but the exact size and shape of the region was unknown.

and continued south, where he discovered a large cape. The body of water narrowed into a strait that ran all the way to the Pacific Ocean. This is now called the Strait of Magellan. Magellan's voyage proved that if land existed below South America, it could only be reached by sea.

In 1577, Queen Elizabeth of England sent Francis Drake to explore potential passages south of South America. Drake sailed around Tierra del Fuego, the southern tip of the continent. He concluded the only thing below South America was ocean. Drake did not travel far enough south to see Antarctica, but the stormy stretch of ocean between Tierra del Fuego and the Antarctic continent is now called the Drake Passage.

As other explorers followed Drake, their reports reshaped the popular fantasy of a rich, warm, mysterious land. Instead the sailors described islands they found in and near the Drake Passage as mountainous, icy, desolate places.

However, some people believed a continent could still exist below these islands. In 1772, England sent James Cook

The Strait of Magellan remained the main passage between the Atlantic Ocean and the Pacific Ocean until the early 1900s.

to solve the mystery. He sailed around southern Africa and continued pushing his ships farther south than anyone had traveled before. Cook crossed the Antarctic Circle. In 1775, he described a rugged island he called South Georgia in

Terror and *Erebus* became stuck in the ice, but their strong hulls allowed them to survive and return to the United Kingdom after Ross's expedition.

honor of King George III: "The inner parts of the country [were] savage and horrible. . . . Not a tree or shrub was to be seen, no not even enough to make a tooth-pick."[1]

Cook returned home convinced there was nothing worthwhile in the far south. But one detail in Cook's reports intrigued some readers. He had taken note of the vast numbers of seals and whales populating the southern seas. The next men to venture south would not be after geographic knowledge. They wanted whale oil and fur.

British sailor Edward Bransfield made the first documented sighting of the continent of Antarctica on January 30, 1820. When the morning haze lifted, Bransfield spotted land to the southwest. He saw the tip of the Antarctic Peninsula, a 1,000-mile (1600 km) stretch of land reaching toward South America.[2]

In October 1839, Royal Navy officer James Clark Ross joined the race for polar glory. He led two ships, *Terror* and *Erebus*, into what is now called the Ross Sea. Ross sailed along the coast of Antarctica in 1841, naming this stretch of land Victoria. Mountains more than 12,000 feet (3,700 m) tall spewed red hot ash and cinder from snow-capped peaks. Ross saw "a perpendicular cliff of ice between 150 and 200 feet above . . . the sea, perfectly flat and level on top."[3] This monstrous hunk of ice, now known as the Ross Ice Shelf, floats beside the continent.

FABIAN VON BELLINGSHAUSEN

Russian explorer Fabian von Bellingshausen was also a key figure in Antarctic exploration, but he is often less recognized among the great polar explorers. In 1819, he sailed south, seeking to fill in the unmapped portions of the southern polar regions. Bellingshausen is overlooked because his journals were not translated into English until 1945. Some historians believe he actually discovered Antarctica before Bransfield did.

THE MADHOUSE

It is one thing to travel to Antarctica to explore then return to civilization, but it is another to actually survive on the frozen continent. The *Belgica*, a Belgian vessel captained by Adrien de Gerlache, became trapped in the Antarctic ice in February 1898. The crew did not break free until

March 1899. In winter below the Antarctic Circle, there is no sunlight for days at a time due to the tilt of the Earth. Seventy days of their imprisonment in the ice were spent in constant darkness.[4]

The ordeal on the *Belgica* trained two of its crew members—Roald Amundsen and Dr. Frederick Cook—to later beat polar records. As the ship remained frozen in the ice, Cook recorded the crew's routine. They drank coffee at 8:00 a.m., exercised at 9:00, and conducted scientific work between 10:00 a.m. and 12:00 p.m. In the afternoon they melted snow for drinking water, repaired instruments, and walked by the moonlight before going to bed at 10:00 p.m. Amundsen said Cook "was the one man of unfaltering courage,

SEAL HUNTING

Furs were big business in the 1700s. Elephant seals, which weigh up to four short tons (3.6 metric tons), were prime targets of hunters. The seals were killed and their hides were hauled up on deck. The meat was tossed into the sea. Big money led to big slaughter. From 1820 to 1822, more than 300,000 seals were killed on the South Shetland Islands alone. One sailor wrote to a New England newspaper in February 1821: "We are now loaded with fur skins, having taken upwards of 18,000 of them. . . . As for getting another cargo in these islands, it is utterly impossible—for there is scarcely a seal left alive."[6]

unfailing hope, endless cheerfulness, and unwearied kindness."[5]

The crew had stocked up on penguin and seal meat to extend their supplies. However, Captain Gerlache, hating the taste of these meats, refused to let them be served. Cook and Amundsen both knew fresh meat prevented scurvy. When crew members began complaining of aching joints, swollen legs, and bleeding gums, Cook ignored the captain and served the sailors fried penguin fillets and seal steaks.

ANTARCTIC CONVERGENCE

When explorers sail to Antarctica they cross a boundary—the Antarctic Convergence. Approximately 930 miles (1,500 km) off the coast of Antarctica, between 50° and 60° south, snakes an underwater barrier.[8] Here, the cold water of the Southern Ocean meets the warmer water of the Indian, Pacific, and Atlantic Oceans. The polar water sinks hundreds of feet below the warmer ocean water and then creeps northward. This boundary surrounds Antarctica, cutting off the continent from warmer ocean water as it swirls in a continuous circle.

As the months of night stretched on, the men's depression grew serious. After one man died, some of the crew insisted the dead man's ghost lingered under the ice. Sideways glances or whistles became signs of evil intent. The ship's meteorologist whispered to Cook, "We are in a mad-house."[7]

The sun reappeared in the spring, but the ship remained locked in the ice only a few thousand feet away from open water. Cook suggested they cut their way out. Day and night for an entire month, the men sawed the ice. By the end of January 1899, they had cut a channel to the sea. The next morning they woke only to discover that the pressure from the pack ice had forced it closed again.

Finally, on March 14, 1899, the ice opened, and a path of open water gave the *Belgica* a chance to escape. The crew raced out before the ice could close again and reached Europe in November. Theirs had been history's first expedition to spend the winter in Antarctica.

Cook, *left*, claimed he reached the North Pole before Peary.

CHAPTER 4

HEROIC JOURNEYS TO THE NORTH

On September 7, 1909, Americans reading the *New York Times* saw a headline proclaiming "Peary Discovers the North Pole after Eight Trials in 23 Years."[1] Readers were confused. Just one week earlier, another paper's headline had read: "The North Pole Discovered by Dr. Cook."[2] Only one man could get to the North Pole first. Who was the true victor? The competition between Peary and Cook remains one of the great controversies in the history of polar exploration.

FIND A WAY OR MAKE ONE

When Robert Edwin Peary was a young naval engineer, he read a book about the exploration of Greenland and discovered his life's ambition. After Fridtjof Nansen crossed the southern region of the Greenland ice cap in 1888, Peary decided he would repeat the journey in the north to discover if Greenland was the highway to the North Pole.

Peary selected seven men for his expedition, including his African-American navigator, Matthew Henson, and Dr. Frederick Cook. Cook was heartbroken from the recent deaths of his wife and baby. For Cook, Peary's call for men to join his expedition "was as if a door to a prison cell had opened. . . . I felt the . . . commanding call of the Northland."[3] This expedition explored hundreds of miles of the Greenland interior. Cook and Peary later went their separate ways. While Cook took an interest in closely studying Arctic peoples, Peary strove single-mindedly for personal glory.

Peary followed the lead of native people in using sled dogs for transport.

EXPLORER IN FOCUS

MATTHEW HENSON

Matthew Henson was a skilled polar explorer. But for years, he received little recognition. He was fluent in the Inuit language and a skilled hunter. He chose the support teams for Peary's North Pole expedition, built the sleds, supervised the sewing of parkas, and trained team members to handle sled dogs and build igloos.

The only credit Peary gave Henson was a compliment on his loyalty and adaptability. Henson did not even receive an invitation to Peary's funeral. However, over the years, Henson's star has risen. In 1948, the National Geographic Society finally awarded Henson a gold medal, and in 1986, a US postage stamp honored him as the first African-American polar explorer.

THE PEARY SYSTEM

Peary returned to the Arctic repeatedly over the next decade, honing his methods. His teams were small. They dressed, ate, and drove dog sleds like the native people. On each expedition, Peary pushed the boundary of exploration northward, but he could not reach the North Pole. On July 6, 1908, at the age of 52, Peary tried one last time. He departed New York City and headed to Canada. There he and his crew spent months in preparation before continuing north in March 1909.

Fifty men and 246 sled dogs relayed supplies ahead of Peary, depositing food and fuel at key spots for use during his return trip. Approximately 134 miles (216 km) from the North Pole, Peary ordered everyone to return to base camp except for four Inuit and Matthew Henson.[4] Later, Peary admitted he wanted to be the only white man on the first expedition to the North Pole.

On April 6, 1909, Henson asked Peary, "We are now at the Pole, are we not?"[5] Peary could not determine the exact location. However, he stuck an American flag atop his igloo.

Peary's expedition left a stone cairn on its way to the North Pole. It was found more than 40 years later by a US Navy arctic supply ship.

The next day Peary took a latitude reading. They were at the North Pole.

Henson and Peary posed for pictures and Peary claimed possession of the North Pole for the United States. Then they turned around and headed south to bask in the glory of victory. Little did Peary know, someone else had already claimed this glory for himself.

COOK'S EXPEDITION

In February 1908, Frederick Cook and nine Inuit set out for the North Pole with 11 sleds pulled by 103 dogs. They left from Annoatok, Greenland, for the 700-mile (1,100 km) journey, much of it over sea ice.[6] Eventually seven of the men turned back. Cook and two Inuit hunters were left to complete the last leg of the trip. On April 21, Cook took a latitude reading and determined they were at the North Pole or as near as they could get on the shifting pack ice. The men buried a brass cylinder in a crevice at the pole to mark their presence.

The return trek to Greenland almost killed Cook and his men. They ran into open water and drifted west on the ice, far from their supply depots. The men wintered for four months in a cave. Finally, by February 1909 the pack ice was solid. On the return march the men survived by hunting

A banquet was held in Cook's honor in New York in September 1909.

and eating their boots. In April 1909, they reached Annoatok. Here Cook met Harry Whitney, an American. Whitney was waiting for a chartered ship to take him home at the end of summer, so he volunteered to bring Cook's trunks of expedition records and navigational instruments home. Then Cook sledded to a southern port and caught a ride on a ship to the United States.

PUBLIC RELATIONS FIGHT

On his way home from his polar expedition, Peary stopped at Annoatok. Whitney informed him Cook claimed to have reached the North Pole in 1908, a full year ahead of Peary. Peary provided Whitney with passage back to the United States on his ship, but he refused to permit any of Cook's property on board. Whitney was forced to hide Cook's trunks among some rocks along the coast. At the telegraph station on Labrador, Peary telegraphed the *New York Times*: "Stars and Stripes nailed to North Pole."[7]

Meanwhile, Cook arrived in New York on September 21, 1909, to thousands of cheering fans. He announced: "I have come from the Pole."[8] When reporters asked to see the sextant he used to determine his latitude at the pole, Cook said it was on route from Greenland. A few days later, Whitney telegraphed Cook informing him Peary had forbidden Whitney to transport Cook's trunks on board his ship. Cook felt sick when he heard this, but he continued giving interviews about his expedition to an adoring public. But soon, Peary began to strike back.

Peary produced testimony from the two Inuit who had accompanied Cook on his polar expedition. They were vague on the details of the trip, though neither man spoke English. The final blow came when the National Geographic Society appointed a three-man committee to investigate Peary's expedition journals. They concluded he had indeed reached the North Pole. Public sentiment swung toward Peary, and the shift took a toll on Cook. He canceled a lecture tour and fled to Europe.

Peary received an elaborate memorial at Arlington National Cemetery, dedicated by the former secretary of the navy, *left*, and Peary's daughter, *right*.

In 1911, Peary appeared before a congressional committee in the United States. He hoped to receive government recognition as the man who discovered the North Pole. But the committee honored Peary as an Arctic explorer who had reached the pole, rather than the man who discovered it. He died nine years later. His gravestone reads: “I shall find a way or make one.”[9]

Controversy remains about who reached the North Pole first. Neither Peary nor Cook used precise instruments for measuring latitude, and some experts doubt either man reached the North Pole at all. What no one can dispute is that both Cook and Peary were courageous explorers who pushed the boundaries of the Arctic world at the dawn of the 1900s.

FLIGHT TO THE NORTH POLE

A trek to the North Pole on water and ice was only one way to reach the explorers' ultimate destination. By the 1920s, a new technology had matured to the point that it could be used in Arctic exploration. The airplane began to unlock new ways to explore the North Pole.

Roald Amundsen had been the first man to reach the South Pole. But by the 1920s, he was a bankrupt 54-year-old with no way to make his dream of flying to the North Pole come true. Then he met Lincoln Ellsworth, the 44-year-old son of a wealthy Chicago businessman. Together, Amundsen and Ellsworth hatched a plan to fly 770 miles (1,200 km) from Spitsbergen, Norway, to the North Pole.[10]

On May 21, 1925, six men in two open-cockpit seaplanes took off into the sky. After seven hours of flight, the men believed they were close to the pole and descended onto the pack ice for a landing. Later Ellsworth said it was like landing in the Grand Canyon: "I have never looked down on a more terrifying place to land an airplane."[11] After rough landings, one plane was beyond repair and the second became locked in the ice. They were still 156 miles (251 km) from the North Pole.[12]

Once the ice thawed, the men realized the ice was too rough to take off again. They were

BURIED ALIVE

In 1930, a British expedition set up a weather station in a remote location on the Greenland ice cap to determine if pilots could fly over the Arctic as part of a mail route. In the winter of 1930–1931, Augustine Courtauld lived alone at the station in a small hut. Air came in through a ventilation tube in the roof. In May 1931, an expedition was sent to relieve Courtauld, but the hut had disappeared. The men on the expedition searched for three weeks and eventually found a few inches of pipe protruding from the snow. They dug a bearded, hollow-faced Courtauld out. Icicles dangled inches from Courtauld's face as he lay in dark. The hut had slowly sunk under the heavy snow. He had been buried alive for five weeks, and his food and fuel supplies were nearly depleted.

400 miles (640 km) from land and had only a one-month supply of food.[13] They would die if they did not build a runway.

They chopped and scraped on their hands and knees trying to level the ice. Time and again they tried to take off. Most of the men despaired. But Amundsen remarked, "When it is darkest, there is always light ahead."[14]

Finally, on June 14, the plane rose from the ice. Seven hours later the team was back in Spitsbergen. Amundsen had made an echo recording proving the ocean beneath the Arctic was so deep there could not be land underneath. But what lay north of their landing site was still a mystery. Determined to

THE *NORGE*

On May 11, 1926, Amundsen, Ellsworth, and Italian pilot Umberto Nobile lifted off in the *Norge* to fly from Norway to Alaska via the North Pole. The *Norge* was an airship 348 feet (106 m) long, 62 feet (19 m) wide, and almost 79 feet (24 m) high. It was essentially a balloon filled with hydrogen contained inside an aluminum frame covered with rubber. The *Norge* could cruise at a speed of approximately 50 miles per hour (80 kmh).[15]

The men reached the North Pole in 15 hours. They dropped Norwegian, American, and Italian flags on the ice and continued on to Alaska. They traveled 2,000 miles (3,200 km) across the Arctic Ocean but did not discover any new land. Ellsworth summed up the significance of the *Norge*: "We had established the scientific fact that the North Polar Region is a vast, deep, ice-covered sea. The white patch on the top of the globe could now be tinted blue."[16]

discover the answer, the men returned the next year in a dirigible called the *Norge*. They flew from Spitsbergen to the North Pole and on to Alaska. Beneath the Arctic ice, they discovered, was nothing but water.

Scott's refusal to rely on dogs would later come back to haunt him in Antarctica.

CHAPTER 5

RACE TO TERRA INCOGNITA

While some men explored the top of the world, others were intrigued by the southernmost areas of the earth. The Antarctic captured the imagination of explorers in the early 1900s. The United Kingdom's Royal Geographic Society appointed Robert Falcon Scott head of the *Discovery* expedition to explore the Antarctic in 1899. He had strong views on the methods explorers should use. Fridtjof Nansen, who led the first expedition across Greenland in 1888, tried to convince Scott sled dogs were the key to success. Scott said: "In my mind no journey ever made with dogs can approach the [greatness] . . . which is realized when a party of men go forth to face hardships, dangers, and difficulties with their own unaided efforts."[1] But Scott agreed to take a few dogs to Antarctica as an experiment.

During the expedition, Scott, his lieutenant Ernest Shackleton, and Dr. Edward Wilson attempted to reach the South Pole. Their dogs became ill and food supplies ran low. The men survived on frozen seal meat and biscuits. Eventually they began to kill and eat their dogs. Scott and Shackleton both suffered from scurvy, and Shackleton was coughing up blood and struggling to breathe. The men turned back and finally reached their ship, the *Discovery*, on February 3, 1900.

The ship was frozen in ice. Scott prepared for another winter in Antarctica, but he ordered Shackleton to return home on a relief ship. That winter Scott and his team explored the mountains of Victoria Land, discovered 500 new species of marine animals, and were the first to retrieve an egg from an emperor penguin rookery. The *Discovery* mission pushed farther south than had any previous expedition. Scott later wrote an account of the expedition, but Shackleton believed Scott portrayed him as weak. Shackleton vowed to return to Antarctica and prove his worth.

RACE TO THE SOUTH POLE

Competition to reach the South Pole began to heat up. In 1910, Scott again made his way south as leader of the British Antarctic Expedition. As he loaded supplies in Australia, Scott received a shocking telegram from Norwegian explorer Roald Amundsen. "Beg to inform you. Fram proceeding Antarctic. Amundsen."[4]

ENDURANCE

In January 1915, Ernest Shackleton's ship, the *Endurance*, froze in the Antarctic pack ice. The explorer had set out in August 1914 to make the first land crossing of Antarctica, but the ice had stopped him from reaching the continent. Months later, the *Endurance* broke up under the immense pressure of the ice and sank. The crew piled into whaleboats and navigated the maze of ice floes. On April 15, 1916, they reached the barren Elephant Island. They had not stood on solid ground since December 5, 1914.

The crew camped on Elephant Island while Shackleton and five others set off for help in one of the whaleboats. Finally, on May 10, 1916, they landed on South Georgia Island. From the shore, the men trekked 20 miles (32 km) over mountains and glaciers to find a whaling station.[2] The whalers stared at the matted, greasy, soot-covered men. "Do you know me?" the men's leader asked. "My name is Shackleton."[3] Rescue was soon dispatched to save the men on South Georgia. Their ordeal had lasted two years. Not a single man died.

Amundsen's dream of becoming the first man to reach the North Pole had been shattered by the exploits of Frederick Cook and Robert Peary in 1909. He decided to aim for the South Pole instead. Amundsen kept his plans secret, not even telling his crew they were heading south instead of north until his ship, the *Fram*, was off the coast of Spain.

The *Fram* reached the Ross Ice Shelf in January 1911, and the crew set up winter camp in the Bay of Whales. Amundsen, eight men, and 46 dogs moved into a hut on the ice and the *Fram* returned home. The explorers placed containers of food and drums of fuel in rustproof containers at a series of supply depots at 80°, 81°, and 82° south. Then the team hunkered down to wait for spring.

Meanwhile, Scott set up camp at McMurdo Sound on the western side of the Ross Ice Shelf. He had three motorized sledges, 19 Siberian ponies, and 32 dogs.[5] Scott and Amundsen prepared differently during the winter.

The *Fram* was specially designed to survive polar ice.

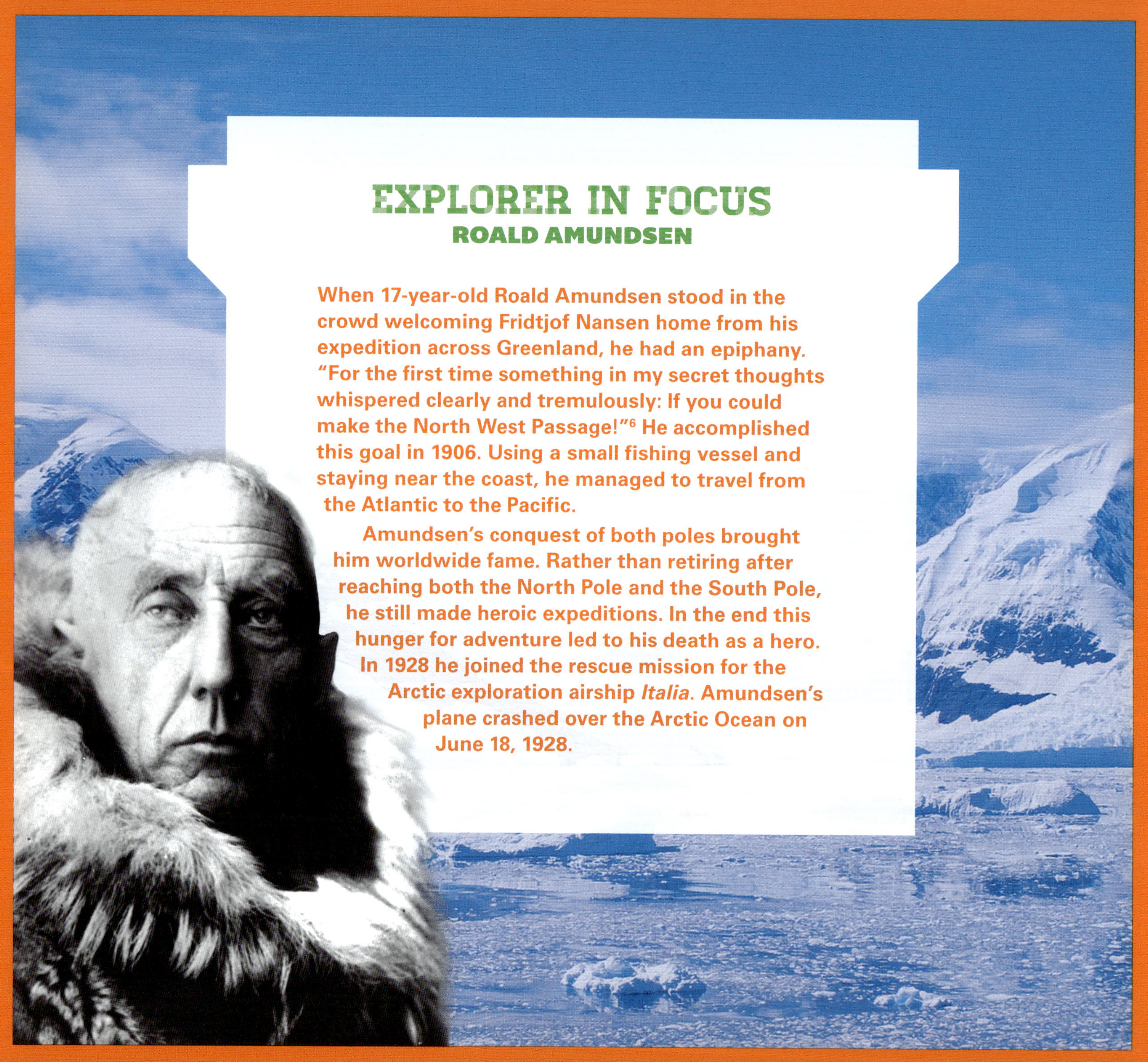

EXPLORER IN FOCUS

ROALD AMUNDSEN

When 17-year-old Roald Amundsen stood in the crowd welcoming Fridtjof Nansen home from his expedition across Greenland, he had an epiphany. "For the first time something in my secret thoughts whispered clearly and tremulously: If you could make the North West Passage!"[6] He accomplished this goal in 1906. Using a small fishing vessel and staying near the coast, he managed to travel from the Atlantic to the Pacific.

Amundsen's conquest of both poles brought him worldwide fame. Rather than retiring after reaching both the North Pole and the South Pole, he still made heroic expeditions. In the end this hunger for adventure led to his death as a hero. In 1928 he joined the rescue mission for the Arctic exploration airship *Italia*. Amundsen's plane crashed over the Arctic Ocean on June 18, 1928.

Amundsen laid out every man's role for the entire expedition in detail. His team took short excursions to test-drive their plans. Using data from these trips, the men redesigned four new sleds, repaired clothing, and enlarged their boots so they could wear extra socks. Amundsen wrote, "Victory awaits him who has everything in order."[7]

In contrast, Scott did not reveal to his crew the identities of the men who would accompany him on the final dash to the pole. He failed to redesign his men's clothing to better suit the harsh climate. Additionally, Scott had an unrealistic schedule. In Antarctica, summer lasts from October to February. Winter lasts from March until September. His plan was to depart on November 3 and return 144 days later on March 27. His return date was in the beginning of winter in the unpredictable Antarctic. Scott's poor planning would have disastrous results.

Spring finally arrived. On October 20, Amundsen, four men, and 55 dogs set out for the pole, 870 miles (1,400 km) away. On skis and sleds they averaged 25 miles (40 km) a day. On November 7, they reached the last supply depot

at 82° south. Beyond this they ran into the Queen Maud Mountains, the boundary between the Ross Ice Shelf and the high Polar Plateau. The terrain rolled like ocean waves, and mountains rose to 15,000 feet (4,600 m). The men's path wound around the mountains until they reached a glacier. They still had 42 dogs left and 350 miles (560 km) to go. Men and dogs clawed their way up the icy glacier. At the top the men killed 24 dogs to feed the remaining dogs. Amundsen admitted, "It was hard but . . . we had agreed to shrink from nothing in order to reach our goal."[8]

The weather turned bad, but the men pushed on. They navigated deadly ridges of ice as they moved toward their destination. The weather cleared on the Polar Plateau, and from there they cruised toward the pole. The men anxiously scanned the area for signs Scott's expedition had arrived first. On the afternoon of December 14, Amundsen cried, "Halt!"[9] They had reached 90° south, and they were

Amundsen took relatively few photographs on his journey, focusing above all else on reaching the pole quickly.

first. The men hoisted the Norwegian flag and raised their frostbitten fists.

For three days the Amundsen team made a variety of measurements to be absolutely certain they were at the pole. They pitched a tent on top of 90° south. Inside they left a note for Scott before heading back to base camp. Amundsen wrote in his diary, "And so, farewell, dear Pole. I don't think we'll meet again."[10] By January 30, 1912, the *Fram* had set sail for home.

DRESSING WARM

People sweat even in below-zero temperatures. If sweat cannot escape an explorer's clothing, it sticks to the skin and turns to ice. James Cook was the first to record concern over what his men wore. He ordered their sleeves lengthened and gave each man a canvas cap. In the 1800s, European explorers wore heavy woolen hats and coats. Amundsen took his lessons from the Inuit to Antarctica in 1912. Reindeer skin trousers, sealskin long underwear, and fur parkas enabled men to work in extreme cold. Today's explorers wear synthetic thermal underwear that wicks moisture away from the skin. A polar fleece or down layer captures warm air. Finally, a windproof outer shell keeps out cold air.

DOOMED EXPLORERS

Meanwhile, the Scott team was having transportation troubles. Because the ponies could not survive the gales and blizzards of early spring, Scott was unable to leave for the pole until the first week in November. Then the motor sledges kept stalling and one by one were abandoned. The ponies fell through the snow. By early December, all the ponies were dead. Then Scott ordered the dogs sent back to base camp, and the team of 12 men harnessed themselves to the sleds. A summer storm made the snow a soupy slush. The men became exhausted, and their sweat-soaked clothes froze at night.

By early January 1912, Scott finally announced who would accompany him to the pole. He ordered all others to return to base camp. Scott had packed only enough food for four men for the final team, but at the last minute he allowed Birdie Bowers to join the group. This last-minute addition was a mistake.

On January 16, the British team spotted a black speck on the horizon. They prayed it was a mirage. The men drew closer and saw the Norwegian team's flag whipping in the wind. Scott wrote, "The POLE. Yes, but under very different circumstances from those expected. We have had a horrible day. . . . Great God! this is an awful place."[11] Inside the tent,

Scott, *center, standing*, was crushed Amundsen had beaten him to the pole.

Scott read Amundsen's note. "If you can use any of the articles left in the tent please do not hesitate to do so. With kind regards I wish you a safe return."[12]

The British team turned around and headed back to civilization on a torturous starvation march. The fuel tins at their supply depots had leaked, and each man experienced serious fatigue and frostbite. They had not had fresh meat for six weeks, and scurvy began to take hold. Edgar Evans's speech slurred, and he could not keep up. On February 17, he slipped into a coma and died.

At one depot, the pony meat they had stored had turned rotten. At another, the supplies were fewer than they needed. In late February, the temperatures dropped to –40° Fahrenheit (–40°C). Their fuel oil was almost gone. Lawrence Oates's feet had turned into blocks of black ice. The team holed up in its tent during a blizzard and Scott recorded the extreme bravery Oates demonstrated. “It was blowing a blizzard. [Oates] said, ‘I am just going outside and may be some time.’”[13] By walking to his certain death, Oates was trying to lessen the burden on the remaining members of the expedition. He was never seen again.

By this time, gangrene had set into Scott’s feet as well. The storm continued, and the men wrote farewell letters. Scott’s message is moving even a century after it was written: “Had we lived, I should have had a tale to tell of the hardihood, endurance and courage of my companions which would have stirred the heart of every Englishman. These rough notes and our dead bodies must tell the tale.”[14]

After Amundsen’s ship reached civilization, the public learned of his conquest. But the world held its breath for news of the British team. Their planned return date, March 27, came and went. Harsh weather prevented any rescue attempt. Finally, on November 12, 1912, searchers found Scott’s tent. The men’s frozen bodies were left on the ice. The commander of the search team said, “Alone in their

A cross was put up in 1913 as a memorial to the lost members of Scott's expedition.

greatness they will lie without change or bodily decay with the most fitting tomb in the world above them."[15]

Wilkins's experience as a photographer in the Australian air force helped him during his Arctic flights.

CHAPTER 6

EXPLORING BY AIR AND BY SEA IN THE ARCTIC

Airplanes and submarines began to replace ponies and dogs as the 1900s continued. However, the new technology did not guarantee success. In 1928, Australian explorer George Hubert Wilkins made the first flight across the Arctic Ocean. Later that year, he flew the first airplane over Antarctica. His next goal took him under the sea instead of into the sky. He planned to cross the Arctic Ocean from Spitsbergen to the Bering Strait by going beneath the North Pole in a submarine.

WHO OWNS THE ARCTIC?

In 1909, Robert Peary planted an American flag near the North Pole. However, on August 2, 2007, a Russian expedition dropped a titanium canister with a Russian flag inside it on the seafloor directly under the North Pole. Russia claimed that this ridge is an extension of its continental shelf, giving the nation rights to that area of the Arctic. The Canadian Foreign Minister said, "You can't go around the world these days dropping a flag somewhere. This isn't the fourteenth or fifteenth century."[1] In 1985, Canada claimed control over the Northwest Passage. Because the islands that line the passage are Canadian, the government claims the passage itself is a Canadian waterway. The United States disagrees. As climate change likely brings the melting of Arctic pack ice, more ships will want to sail over the roof of the world. International disputes over this issue will likely grow worse in the coming decades.

Wilkins rented a retired submarine from the US Navy and renamed it the *Nautilus*. His expedition set off from New York on June 4, 1931. Almost immediately, heavy weather damaged both of the vessel's main engines and the sub docked in Ireland for repairs. When the submarine finally reached the Arctic pack ice on August 11, the expedition was three months behind schedule. Then Wilkins attempted some short submerged trips but discovered the submarine was unable to dive. He did not have the money for repairs. Wilkins returned to

Norway, and on November 30, 1931, the *Nautilus* was towed offshore and sunk.

GLOBAL MASTERS

As conflict between nations escalated in the first half of the 1900s, governments eyed the Arctic corridor. They believed control of this route atop the world would bring with it significant international influence. Pilots from the Soviet Union were the first to land on the North Pole in 1937. They wanted Arctic flights to improve the connections between the Soviet Union's Pacific and northern naval fleets.

International cooperation over the Arctic became critical during World War II (1939–1945). The United States, the United

ICEBREAKERS

After World War II, steel ships replaced wooden ones. Then a new type of ship was invented specially for polar travel: icebreakers. The hulls of icebreakers have extremely strong frames and steel plates more than twice the thickness of those on regular ships. With specially designed bows, they ride up on the ice and use their weight to crush it. Icebreakers are designed without extra fittings on their hull, such as a keel, to avoid getting caught on the ice. However, this has a tendency to make them roll easily on the open ocean. Despite their bulk, icebreakers can maneuver quickly to avoid icebergs. Many are also equipped with a flight deck for helicopters.

Kingdom, and the Soviet Union allied to defeat Nazi Germany. The United Kingdom and the United States used Arctic sea and air routes to resupply Soviet forces fighting against the German army.

The end of World War II also ended the cooperation between the United States and the Soviet Union. The Cold War, a period of hostility between the two powers, would continue through the next four decades. No actual shots were fired, but competition for influence drove both sides to explore, conduct science, and develop the military forces of the future. One of the places they faced off was in the Arctic. As US general Henry H. Arnold said, "If World War III should come, its strategic center will be the North Pole."[2]

In 1946, the United States sent B-29 bombers over the Arctic. The government claimed these were weather research missions, but in reality the crews were searching for any undiscovered

During World War II, the Soviet military faced harsh Arctic conditions on its northern battlefields and seas.

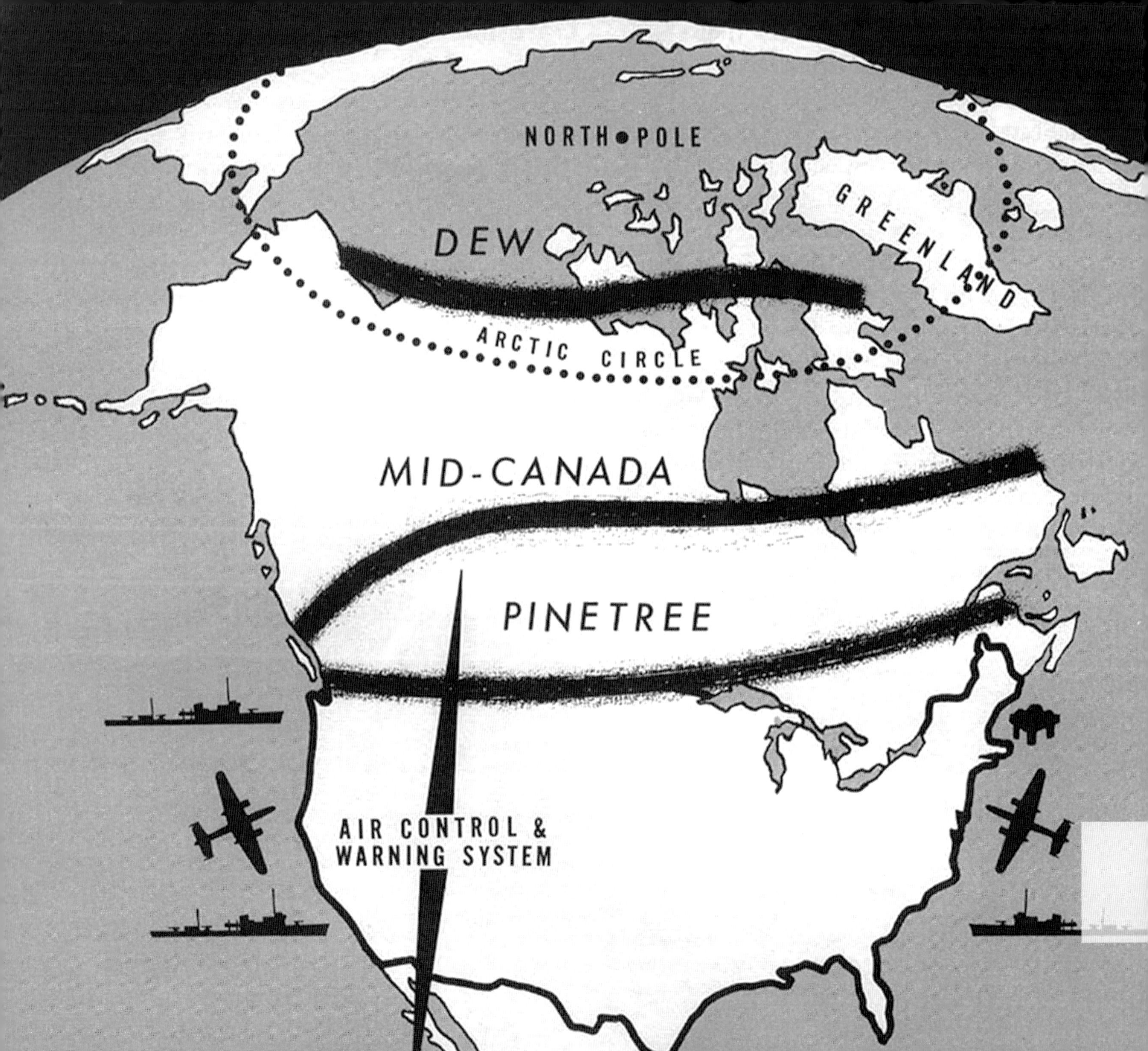

NORTH POLE
GREENLAND
DEW
ARCTIC CIRCLE
MID-CANADA
PINETREE
AIR CONTROL &
WARNING SYSTEM

land in the Arctic that could be used for military bases. No new land was found, but ice islands were discovered. One of these, Fletcher Island, was used as a weather and spy station to eavesdrop on the Soviets.

On September 3, 1949, the United States detected abnormally high levels of radioactive debris in the atmosphere. Before that time the United States was the only country that possessed nuclear bombs. The radiation levels showed this monopoly had ended. The data proved the Soviets had just successfully tested a nuclear bomb. Cities in the United States were now vulnerable to a Soviet attack. A bomber attack was likely to come via the most direct route from the Soviet Union to the United States—over the North Pole. To safeguard against this possibility, the United States and Canada cooperated in combined military exercises in the Arctic.

The US military presence physically changed the Arctic. The Distant Early Warning (DEW) Line was

The DEW Line was the northernmost of three defensive lines maintained by the United States and Canada during the Cold War.

constructed across 3,000 miles (4,800 km) of the North American Arctic. This line of radar stations would alert the United States to any Soviet attacks. Six main stations were set up at 500-mile (800 km) intervals with secondary stations every 100 miles (161 km). More than 46,000 short tons (42,000 metric tons) of steel were used in construction. The amount of gravel used could have built a two-lane road stretching from Florida to California. More than 20,000 construction workers lived in the Arctic from 1952 to 1957.[3] To make room for an American airbase on Thule in Greenland, the local Inuit were forcibly relocated.

Military concerns also led to scientific exploration in the Arctic. In 1960 the US Army Polar Research and Development Center

RELOCATION OF THE INUIT

In 1953, the Canadian government engaged in an action that remained hidden for four decades. Canada wanted to stake a claim to the islands of the northern Arctic. So the government relocated Inuit people in many of these locations. In one case, dozens of Inuit people were moved from their homes in Port Harrison to barren, rocky Resolute Bay on Cornwallis Island. This island was cold but there was little snow to build igloos. The supply of food was limited, and Inuit families had to scavenge scraps from the garbage of the air force base on the island. For decades they were denied the right to return home. The Canadian government finally paid settlements to survivors and their families in the 1990s. It issued a formal apology in 2008.

built a miniature city on the ice cap of Greenland. Camp Century was built under the ice and became home to more than 100 scientists and soldiers. Their mission was to find ways to live in the fierce climate. Nuclear power fueled the city. Main Street was 1,100 feet (330 m) long, and 21 tunnels branched from it. Residents had access to a kitchen, a dining room, and a communication center. The scientists drilled 4,500 feet (1,400 m) down into the ice cap, extracting fragments of ice laid down thousands of years ago to study climate changes.[4]

However, even the technological skill of the United States could not defeat the fierce conditions of the Arctic. The tunnel roof was unable to withstand the pressure from heavy snowfall. Ice accumulated on the insides of the tunnel walls and ceiling. Residents had to use a chainsaw to shave it down so they could walk through. Camp Century was eventually abandoned.

The *Skate* surfaced at the North Pole again on March 17, 1959.

EXPLORING THE ARCTIC SEAFLOOR

The competition between the United States and the Soviet Union entered outer space in 1957 when the Soviet Union launched Sputnik, the first artificial satellite to orbit the earth. However, the United States did not give up the Arctic in the space age. In 1957, the United States sent the world's first nuclear-powered submarine, the *Nautilus*, to the Arctic. The name *Nautilus* had long been used for submarines in both reality and fiction. It explored the waters beneath the ice. In 1958, another US nuclear submarine, the *Skate*, finally fulfilled Wilkins's vision when it surfaced at the North Pole on August 11. Wilkins's ashes were scattered to the winds and the Australian flag was hoisted in his honor.

Today, after the end of the Cold War, Arctic exploration is usually about scientific inquiry rather than military advantage. In 2007, the Woods Hole Oceanographic Institute led an expedition of 60 scientists on a 40-day journey to study the seafloor of the Arctic. They explored the Gakkel Ridge, a seam that runs across the ocean floor in the Arctic between North America and Asia. The Swedish icebreaker *Oden* plowed its way through pack ice, and its helicopters ferried scientists from the ship to locations they wanted to study.

Modern explorers use a device called a camera and sampler (CAMPER) to collect information about the seafloor. The CAMPER is lowered into the water. Cameras capture footage from beneath the ice, while hoses use suction to collect samples. Researchers also use autonomous underwater vehicles (AUVs) to explore the Arctic waters. AUVs are robotic submarines that propel themselves along the ocean floor on preprogrammed routes, collecting images and other data.

Modern Arctic expeditions often deploy buoys to collect data remotely.

SCIENCE AT THE NORTH POLE

The ice over the North Pole is always drifting, so studying it remains a technical challenge. Unlike the South Pole, where scientists live in miniature cities, no permanent facilities can be built on drifting ice. However, since 2000, an international team has launched annual spring expeditions to the North Pole. They established a series of unmanned scientific observatories to collect data on the salinity of the ocean water and the thickness of the ice cover.

This kind of work takes a special kind of explorer: part scientist to collect and understand polar research data, part mechanic to fix things that break thousands of miles from repair shops, and part athlete to survive the brutal conditions. And these scientists have to work fast. The ice floes they stand on can drift or break without warning. If rough

LIFE IN THE ARCTIC OCEAN

Video from the floor of the Arctic Ocean reveals a world from science fiction. Undersea volcanoes release steam. A species of octopus propels through the water by flapping large ear-like appendages. Masses of yellow bacteria cling to rocks and thrive in this dark, frigid world. Exploring the variety of life in the Arctic waters will keep scientists busy for decades.

weather suddenly closes in, helicopter pilots may be unable to reach science groups working on the ice. One scientist said there are three rules to working in the Arctic: “Never pass up a meal, never pass up a shower, and never pass up a flight south.”[5]

Shackleton's *Endurance* expedition left days after World War I broke out. The crew became stranded in Antarctica until 1916.

CHAPTER 7

CONFLICT AND COMPROMISE IN ANTARCTICA

Only a few years after the Antarctic explorations of Amundsen and Scott, Europe plunged into World War I (1914–1918), and virtually all expeditions to Antarctica halted. Once peace was restored in 1918, exploration began again. New technologies that saw dramatic advances as a result of the war, including airplanes and radios, revolutionized Antarctic exploration. Another factor also had an effect on the world's relationship with Antarctica—changing global politics.

TAKING TO THE SKIES

On November 16, 1928, Australian George Hubert Wilkins set off to fly across Antarctica. His 2,000-mile (3,200 km) flight would not pass directly over the South Pole. The remoteness of the pole proved too risky for early airplanes. Instead, he would fly a shorter, safer route over the continent. Wilkins's first attempt lasted only 20 minutes, but it was a first. Then on December 20, he and copilot Ben Eielson flew for ten hours and traveled 1,200 miles (1,900 km) over land that had never been seen before.[1] Wilkins named landmarks for the wealthy individuals who had sponsored his journey, and he dropped documents that claimed the land for the British.

American aviator Richard Byrd followed Wilkins. In 1928, he established a permanent camp on the Bay of Whales called Little America. Then, in the fall of 1929, Byrd made a round-trip flight from Little America to the South Pole.

It took a great deal of money to finance a flight in Antarctica. US millionaire Lincoln Ellsworth, who had previously flown with Amundsen, had both the money and the desire. In 1933, he purchased a Northrop Gamma cargo plane and named it the *Polar Star*. His goal was to fly 3,400 miles (5,500 km) from the Ross Sea to the Weddell Sea and back.[2] One problem after another delayed his takeoff in October 1934. Squalls hit. There were engine problems. The icy runway melted. Finally on January 3, 1935, the *Polar Star* lifted off with Ellsworth and his pilot, Bernt Balchen. An hour into the flight Balchen had second thoughts.

ALONE ON THE ICE

In 1934, Richard Byrd manned a weather station alone on the Ross Ice Shelf over the winter. Each day, he went outside and recorded weather data. By May, the temperature had dropped to −96 degrees Fahrenheit (−71°C). Winds jammed snow into the weather instruments. One day, Byrd crawled outside in a blizzard to clear the instruments, and the door froze shut behind him, locking him outside. "I clawed at the three-foot square of timber like a madman," he remembered. "I beat on it with my fists."[3]

Eventually, Byrd pried the trapdoor open. But soon after, his generator malfunctioned and carbon monoxide began leaking in. Byrd realized he was slowly being poisoned, but he did not want to request a rescue mission that would risk the lives of other men. From Byrd's rambling radio messages, the men at base camp knew something was wrong. As soon as the weather improved, they rescued him.

The *Polar Star* can now be seen at the National Air and Space Museum in Washington, DC.

He turned around the plane and returned to base. He said, "Ellsworth can commit suicide if he likes, but he can't take me with him."[4]

That was the end of that exploration season. Ellsworth had already spent $150,000 and had nothing to show for it. But he was determined. Back in the United States, he vowed to cross Antarctica by air.

Ellsworth returned to Antarctica in 1935 with a new pilot, Canadian Herbert Hollick-Kenyon. The men set off on November 22, 1935. On December 5, as the men saw the Ross Sea in the distance, the *Polar Star* ran out of fuel. The plane sputtered and glided to a landing. They were unsure of exactly where the base camp was. They wandered for ten days, hauling their sleds for 100 miles (161 km) before they finally found the camp. It had been only 16 miles (26 km) from the plane.[5]

WORLD WAR II

As World War II raged, many nations tried to claim Antarctica. The British navy took over abandoned whaling stations to guard against German aggression. Argentina deposited a bronze cylinder on Deception Island with a document inside that claimed specific lands. The Argentines also painted their flag on the walls of an old whaling station. In response, the British navy removed the Argentine cylinder, painted over the Argentine flag, and hoisted a British flag.

These punches and counterpunches continued. As part of Operation Tabarin, the United Kingdom set up three bases at which crews conducted some exploration and some research. But their presence was really about politics. The thinking went that the nation occupying the land was the nation that owned the land.

OPERATION HIGHJUMP

In November 1946, the United States sent a massive expedition to Antarctica. Thirteen ships, 23 planes, and

Operation Highjump included some of the earliest exploration of Antarctica using helicopters.

4,700 men arrived on the Antarctic Peninsula.[6] The men made survey flights and dropped documents over lands that had already been claimed by the United Kingdom, Argentina, and Chile. The goal of this mission was to build up a US presence in Antarctica and scout locations for permanent bases and airfields.

Operation Highjump lasted only one year and accomplished little. The men mapped only a fourth of the region they had intended to chart. More than half of the photographs they took were useless. However, Highjump did establish the United States as having the most formidable military presence in Antarctica.

OPERATION DEEPFREEZE

During the International Geophysical Year, the United States committed to coordinating its military resources with other nations to set up seven bases staffed by scientists. This first phase of Operation Deepfreeze set up McMurdo Station on Ross Island and Little America V on the Ross Ice Shelf. The second phase constructed the Amundsen-Scott base at the South Pole and the Byrd Station 650 miles (1,000 km) inland from the original Little America. The final phase of Deepfreeze included men wintering over at the seven US research bases. They gathered seismic readings and meteorological data and discovered the ice cap at the South Pole was almost 9,000 feet (2,700 m) thick.[7]

THE INTERNATIONAL GEOPHYSICAL YEAR

As politicians squabbled in the 1940s and 1950s, scientists cooperated. Scientists around the world had already held two International Polar Years, in 1882 and in 1932. These events focused the attention of scientists

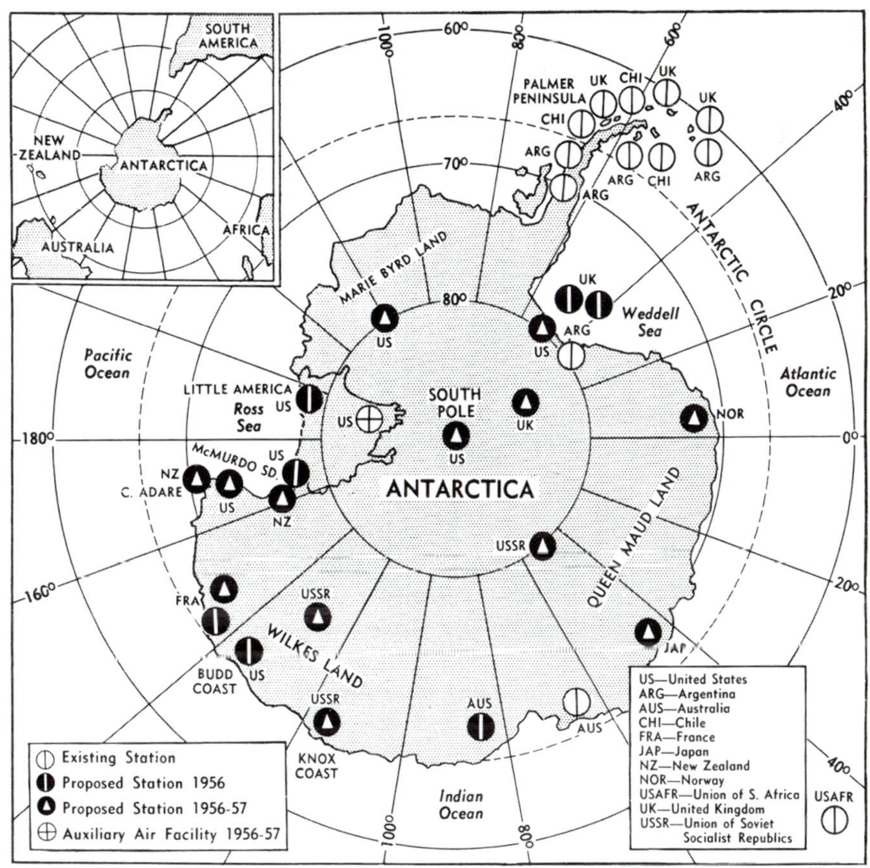

More than two dozen Antarctic research bases participated in the IGY.

around the world on particular subjects. The third and most ambitious polar year was called the International Geophysical Year (IGY) and focused largely on Antarctica. It lasted from July 1957 to December 1958. Twelve nations participated.

MISSION IN FOCUS
THE COMMONWEALTH TRANS-ANTARCTIC EXPEDITION

In 1957, Vivian Fuchs led the Commonwealth Trans-Antarctic Expedition across Antarctica. Four nations—Australia, the United Kingdom, New Zealand, and South Africa—provided financial support.

On November 24, 1957, ten men, three snowmobiles, a tractor, and dog teams headed out. Thirty miles (48 km) into the trek, a field of crevasses greeted the team. A warm spell had weakened the ice bridges over these chasms. Fuchs recalled these crevasses were like "traps deliberately set."[8] It took the team almost one month to cross this field.

Next, the team faced a 555-mile (893 km) march to the South Pole. Wind-hardened ridges exhausted them. At times they could travel only a few miles a day. On January 19, 1958, the party reached the top of a ridge. Below them lay "a small cluster of huts and radio masts."[9] It was the Amundsen-Scott South Pole Station. There the men rested for a few days, enjoying hot showers and cold drinks. Then they set off for McMurdo Sound.

Antarctica had finally been crossed on foot. In some ways, the expedition signaled the end of an era. New technology was expensive. Science, not personal glory, was the new goal of Antarctic expeditions. Only governments had the wealth and power to back these advanced explorations.

Dozens of bases were set up in Antarctica and more than 5,000 scientists worked on the continent. Among the most important discoveries made during the IGY involved the Filchner Ice Shelf. An expedition traveled 1,200 miles (1,900 km) across the shelf and studied the mountains south of it.[10] Scientists explored the structure of the shelf and the seabed beneath it and discovered part of the shelf was actually an island.

WOMEN ON THE ICE

The first two women to winter in Antarctica did not intend to. In 1947, Jackie Ronne and Jennie Darlington accompanied their husbands to Chile, intending to return home when their spouses headed to Antarctica. At the last minute, Ronne's husband decided she should join the expedition to help with clerical work. Darlington's husband informed her she was drafted too.

In 1956, Russian scientist Marie Klenova participated in a team charting the coast of Antarctica. For many years, the US Navy and the National Science Foundation prohibited American women from working on the continent. Finally, in 1969, the first female scientists were allowed to submit research proposals and join the US Antarctic Program. Today approximately one-third of the scientists who work at McMurdo Station are women.[11]

ANTARCTIC TREATY

At the end of the IGY, scientists hoped international cooperation in Antarctica could continue. In May 1958, US President Dwight D. Eisenhower sent a letter to 11 other nations stating Antarctica should "be used only for peaceful purposes."[12] Representatives from several countries held 60 secret meetings, and in 1961 the Antarctic Treaty became international law, establishing the continent as a shared resource.

Over the years, the treaty has been expanded and amended, and now 50 nations have signed it.[13] Freedom of science rules in Antarctica. No military activity is allowed. Nuclear testing and dumping of nuclear waste are prohibited. Member nations can inspect each other's stations. The Antarctic Treaty has no expiration date.

CALLING HOME

Communications technology came slowly to polar regions. When Amundsen and Scott made their famous dash for the South Pole, the world had to wait weeks for the news of who won. Months passed before news of Scott's death was certain. When Shackleton's men battled disasters on the *Endurance* expedition, they were oblivious to the fact World War I had begun. Radio was not routinely used in Antarctica until the 1940s, and even then it was not always reliable. By the 1960s, satellite technology opened Antarctica to the world. Phone, fax, and e-mail are used routinely at the bases in Antarctica today.

Tourists now visit Arctic and Antarctic landscapes once reserved for risk-taking explorers.

CHAPTER 8

THE FUTURE OF POLAR EXPLORATION

Today, tourism, science, resources, and adventure drive polar exploration. Tours to the Arctic are educational as well as leisure oriented. Most Arctic travel goes to Greenland, Spitsbergen, and Baffin Island. But these trips are not for the low-budget traveler. Flights to the North Pole cost upwards of $5,000 and a trip on a Russian icebreaker can break the bank at $18,000 per person.[1]

Adventure-seeking tourists have traveled to Antarctica since the 1950s. Most tourists view the harsh beauty of the land from their floating hotel rooms on cruise ships. The Antarctic Treaty regulates where tourists can go and how they can travel. People who want to set foot on the continent are required to land on light inflated boats called Zodiacs, and nearly all tours are restricted to the Antarctic Peninsula. The number of tourists to Antarctica continues to rise.

Some experts predict in the future an airfield will be built on King George Island. Then tourists could fly across the Drake Passage, eliminating days of rough sea travel. This would likely increase the number of tourists and open up more areas of the Antarctic Peninsula. Regulation

CHANGING LIVES OF THE INUIT

Over the last two decades, native people have been asserting their rights across the Arctic. Canadian Inuit signed a treaty with the Canadian government in 1993. They received $1.17 billion dollars in compensation for the loss of their traditional lands.[2] Additionally, the Canadian government created a province for the Inuit—Nunavut. However, this homeland cannot restore their traditional ways. While the elders still hunt and fish, the younger generation watches television and buys food from convenience stores. Arctic settlements are full of people caught between the old world and the new.

Antarctic tourism is currently limited to the area around the Antarctic Peninsula, but future developments could open more of the continent to visitors.

will need to be strengthened to maintain this last pristine place on earth.

MELTING ICE

Ice at the top and bottom of the world is melting. Climate change is the biggest threat to the future of the poles and

Melting ice at the poles can lead to the calving, or breaking apart, of huge glaciers.

is the focus of polar exploration today. In April 2012, the US National Research Council released its conclusions from the data gathered during the 2007–2008 International Polar Year. Seven out of the twelve ice shelves that line the

Antarctic Peninsula are gone or almost gone. Certain kinds of plankton have been discovered in North Atlantic waters where they have not lived for 800,000 years.[3] These findings demonstrated the dramatic changes brought about by melting polar ice.

The year 2012 set a new record for Arctic sea ice melt. The condition of the remaining ice has changed, too. Permanent ice floes have shrunk and thinner, weaker ice has replaced them. This means strong spring and summer winds can break these thinner ice floes apart, allowing them to melt more easily. Less ice means more ocean is exposed to heat from the sun. The water absorbs the heat, warming the ocean. These changes in Arctic sea ice have been tentatively linked to more violent storm activity around the world.

CLIMATE CHANGE AND THE ARCTIC

Those who live in the Arctic recognize their land is changing as the Earth grows warmer. Veteran explorer Will Steger walked 1,000 miles (1,600 km) over 78 days in the Inuit province of Nunavut to listen to the native people describe what they see.[5] Robins, finches, and dolphins, animals that do not typically live in the Arctic, are now spotted regularly. Changing wind patterns have transformed ice landmarks the locals have used for navigation for centuries.

Scientists are currently studying the Ross Ice Shelf. They hope to predict how long it would take the ice shelf to melt if the climate continues to warm. The Ross Ice Shelf holds the ice of West Antarctica in place, much like a cork in a bottle. If the ice shelf disappears, West Antarctica's glaciers will flow faster to the ocean and could raise sea levels by up to 20 feet (6 m) in a matter of centuries.[4] Scientists continue their work in the Antarctic to refine their predictions of how the melting ice might affect the planet and its climate.

AN ICE-FREE NORTHWEST PASSAGE?

The hunt for a water route from Europe to Asia drove explorers into the Arctic for centuries. The passage was eventually found, but it is dangerous, expensive, and only ice-free for a few months in certain years. But some climatologists have suggested global temperature increases may melt the ice of the Northwest Passage, opening it to year-round shipping by 2030.

Pipelines and other signs of resource-gathering infrastructure are becoming more and more visible in the Arctic.

A potential problem with an ice-free Northwest Passage is the fact countries disagree on who would own such a lucrative route. Canada has long said the Northwest Passage is an internal route that belongs to it. The United States and the European Union insist these are international waters. This issue is not just political but also financial.

The Arctic is estimated to hold 13 percent of the world's untapped oil reserves and one-third of its natural gas.[6] Iceland, Russia, Canada, the United States, and the Scandinavian countries have formed the Arctic Council to resolve disputes and regulate conduct in the Arctic. Other countries have recently begun to flex their global weight. China and seven other Asian nations have recently been granted observer status in the Arctic Council. At the present there are no legal guidelines for resolving disputes between nations wanting to explore for Arctic wealth.

PHYSICS IN ANTARCTICA

Unique scientific research can be conducted at the poles. This includes research on subatomic particles called neutrinos. Scientists can measure neutrinos but cannot see them because neutrinos pass through matter without being affected. That is where the Antarctic Muon and Neutrino Detection Array (AMANDA) comes in. AMANDA is a telescope with 670 light sensors built into pressure-resistant glass spheres. Hundreds of these spheres have been attached to steel cables and sunk one mile (1.6 km) into the Antarctic ice. AMANDA can see where the human eye cannot. When a neutrino collides with a molecule of ice, it emits a flash of blue light, gone in less than one billionth of a second. AMANDA can spot these flashes and relay information to scientists on the surface.

THE COLDEST JOURNEY

Explorers have walked on, flown over, and sailed to the Arctic and Antarctic. They are no longer blank places on the map of the earth. The explorers of today are engineers, mechanics, scientists, and pilots. They are men and women from all regions of the world.

However, the human spirit has not changed so much in the last few centuries. Some brave souls still desire to pit their bodies and spirits against the harshest lands on earth. These are the polar adventurers.

On December 6, 2012, a six-man team left England to go on what some have dubbed "the last remaining polar challenge."[7] Their goal: trek 2,000 miles (3,200 km) across Antarctica in the winter. They intended to gather scientific information and elevate the United Kingdom back to its status as home of the world's greatest polar explorers.

This expedition was full of symbolism for the British. The year it began, 2012, marked the 100-year anniversary of Robert Falcon Scott's expedition to the South Pole. Sir Ranulph Fiennes, one of the most accomplished explorers of the modern age, led the team.

The expedition was dangerous. During the Antarctic winter, the team would travel for three months in complete

Seeing is Believing
FINNING
Seeing is Believing

darkness. They had a specially designed tractor to pull a supply train containing the men's fuel and supplies. They planned to be completely self-sufficient for eight months. However, in February 2013, Fiennes developed frostbite and had to be evacuated. The rest of the team vowed to finish. In June 2013, the expedition was halted. A huge field of icy crevasses made movement too difficult. Even with modern technology, polar exploration still presents a daunting challenge to explorers.

Competition still exists among polar explorers. When Fiennes was interviewed before the expedition left, he said he had heard the Norwegians were planning an attempt to cross Antarctica in the winter. In 1912, the Norwegian Roald Amundsen beat Robert Scott to the South Pole. When Fiennes heard the rumor he knew the British team had to try first.

Many people wonder what motivates people to go to these extreme places and subject themselves to the

Fiennes was forced to turn back when his hand was damaged by frostbite.

Even today, the allure of polar exploration continues to attract explorers from all over the world.

possibility of injury and death. Fiennes's answer: "Sometimes we don't succeed, but it's what we go for. It's our specialty."[8] These polar explorers, like all those who came before them, seek to test their limits and find adventure at the ends of the earth.

TIMELINE

325 BCE Pytheas records the first journey to the Arctic.

874 CE The Vikings colonize Iceland.

1519 Ferdinand Magellan discovers a strait at the bottom of South America.

1576 Martin Frobisher sails to the Arctic and finds the bay later named after him.

1728 Vitus Bering locates the Bering Strait and concludes North America and Asia are not connected.

1775 James Cook sails below the Antarctic Circle and lands on South Georgia Island.

1820 On January 30, Edward Bransfield records the first sighting of Antarctica.

1841 James Clark Ross discovers the Ross Ice Shelf.

1845 In May, John Franklin's expedition sets out to explore the Arctic Archipelago and vanishes.

1871 The first US expedition to the Arctic, the *Polaris*, sets sail on June 29.

1908 Frederick Cook claims he reached the North Pole on April 21.

1909 Robert Peary and Matthew Henson claim they reached the North Pole on April 6.

1911 On December 14, a Norwegian expedition led by Roald Amundsen is the first to reach the South Pole.

1926 The *Norge* departs on the first flight over the North Pole on May 11.

1929 Richard Byrd flies over the South Pole.

1957 The Commonwealth Trans-Antarctic Expedition begins a trek across Antarctica on November 24.

1958 The *Skate*, a US submarine, surfaces at the North Pole on August 11.

1961 On June 23, the Antarctica Treaty goes into effect.

1993 Canadian Inuit sign a treaty with the Canadian government.

2012 On December 6, a polar expedition sets out from the United Kingdom in an attempt to cross Antarctica during winter.

ESSENTIAL FACTS ABOUT POLAR EXPLORATION

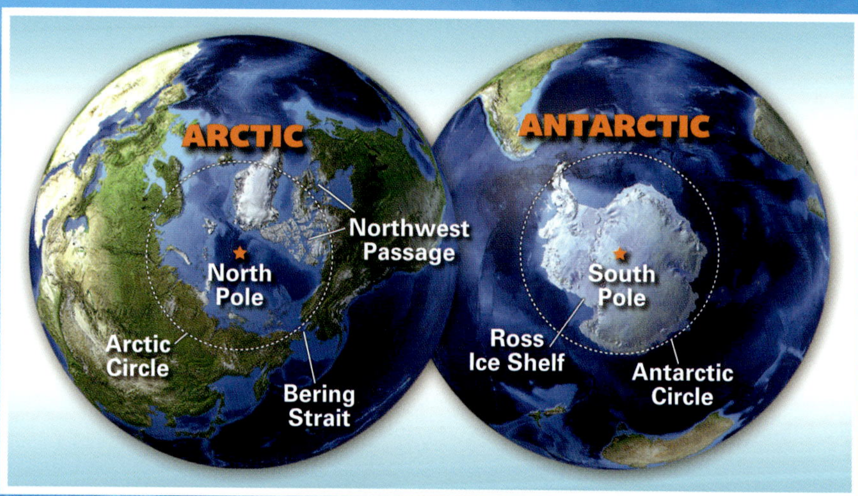

KEY DISCOVERIES AND THEIR IMPACTS

In 1820, Edward Bransfield recorded the first sighting of the continent of Antarctica.

In 1841, James Clark Ross discovered the Ross Ice Shelf. The Ross Ice Shelf was the launching point for expeditions to the South Pole and is home to permanent scientific research stations today.

Data from the 2007–2008 International Polar Year revealed Arctic pack ice is melting quickly, a symptom of global warming.

KEY PLAYERS

James Cook sailed to the Arctic and Antarctic for the United Kingdom in the 1770s.

Frederick Cook and Robert Peary both claimed to reach the North Pole. The issue remains controversial.

Roald Amundsen was the first to navigate the Northwest Passage and was part of the team that flew across the Arctic.

Robert Falcon Scott and Roald Amundsen competed in a brash race to lead the first expedition to the South Pole in 1911.

KEY TECHNOLOGY

Explorers learned to use the fur clothing and sled dogs used by the native people in the Arctic.

Icebreaker ships and specially designed aircraft allowed explorers and scientists to travel farther and more safely in polar regions.

Radio and satellite communications made it possible to coordinate expeditions from faraway bases.

QUOTE

"I shall find a way or make one."

—Robert Peary

GLOSSARY

archipelago
A group of islands.

cairn
A mound of stones used as a marker.

crevasse
A deep crack in a glacier.

dirigible
An airship; a kind of balloon with an internal frame that is propelled by a motor and can be steered.

emissary
A person sent on a mission to represent another person or organization.

gangrene
The death of body tissue from a lack of blood supply.

ice cap
A thick sheet of ice covering a large area of land.

ice floe
A large thin sheet of ice floating in the sea.

ice shelf
A broad, flat area of an ice cap that extends over the sea but remains attached to land.

icebreaker
A sturdy ship built for navigating through icebound waters.

Inuit
A member of a group of native people who live in the Arctic.

kayak
A lightweight boat propelled by a double-bladed paddle.

pack ice
Sea ice in the polar regions that floats on the ocean.

quinine
A medicine used to treat fever.

salinity
Saltiness.

sextant
A navigational instrument used to determine longitude and latitude.

sound
A long and wide body of water that is larger than a strait and connects larger bodies of water.

tundra
A treeless region where the subsoil is permanently frozen.

ADDITIONAL RESOURCES

SELECTED BIBLIOGRAPHY

Encounters at the End of the World. Dir. Werner Herzog. Image Entertainment, 2008. Film.

Lainema, Matti, and Nurminen, Juha. *A History of Arctic Exploration: Discovery, Adventure and Endurance at the Top of the World*. New York: Sterling, 2009. Print

Landis, Marilyn J. *Antarctica: Exploring the Extreme—Four Hundred Years of Adventure*. Chicago: Chicago Review, 2001. Print.

Wilkinson, Alec. *The Ice Balloon: S. A. Andrée and the Heroic Age of Arctic Exploration*. New York: Knopf, 2011. Print.

FURTHER READINGS

Bredeson, Carmen. *After the Last Dog Died: The True-Life, Hair-Raising Adventure of Douglas Mawson and his 1911–1914 Antarctic Expedition*. Washington, DC: National Geographic, 2003. Print.

Linder, Chris. *Science on Ice: Four Polar Expeditions*. Chicago: U of Chicago P, 2011. Print.

Meyers, Walter Dean. *Antarctica: Journeys to the South Pole*. New York: Scholastic, 2004. Print.

WEB SITES

To learn more about exploring polar regions, visit ABDO Publishing Company online at **www.abdopublishing.com**. Web sites about exploring polar regions are featured on our Book Links page. These links are routinely monitored and updated to provide the most current information available.

FOR MORE INFORMATION

For more information on this subject, contact or visit the following organizations:

The Peary-MacMillan Arctic Museum
9500 College Street
Brunswick, ME 04011
207-725-3416
http://www.bowdoin.edu/arctic-museum/information/index.shtml
This museum highlights the Arctic voyages of Robert Peary and has a full collection of artifacts representing the Inuit culture.

The Woods Hole Oceanographic Institute
266 Woods Hole Road
Woods Hole, MA 02543
508-289-2252
http://www.whoi.edu/main/contact-us
This institute is dedicated to researching and understanding the oceans. Polar research is one of its ongoing areas of study and exploration.

SOURCE NOTES

CHAPTER 1. MURDER, MAYHEM, AND MUTINY IN THE ARCTIC

1. Bruce Henderson. *Fatal North: Adventure and Survival Aboard USS* Polaris, *the First US Expedition to the North Pole*. New York: New American Library, 2001. Print. 28.

2. "Smith Sound." *Encyclopaedia Britannica*. Encyclopaedia Britannica, 2013. Web. 28 Aug. 2013.

3. Bruce Henderson. *Fatal North: Adventure and Survival Aboard USS* Polaris, *the First US Expedition to the North Pole*. New York: New American Library, 2001. Print. 71.

4. "Arctic Ocean." *Encyclopaedia Britannica*. Encyclopaedia Britannica, 2013. Web. 28 Aug. 2013.

5. "Compare the Poles." *Polar Discovery*. Woods Hole Oceanographic Institution, 2006. Web. 26 Apr. 2013.

6. "Which Pole is Colder?" *Climate Kids*. NASA, n.d. Web. 28 Aug. 2013.

7. Bruce Henderson. *Fatal North: Adventure and Survival Aboard USS* Polaris, *the First US Expedition to the North Pole*. New York: New American Library, 2001. Print. 145.

8. Ibid. 148.

9. "North Pole." *Encyclopaedia Britannica*. Encyclopaedia Britannica, 2013. Web. 28 Aug. 2013.

10. Bruce Henderson. *Fatal North: Adventure and Survival Aboard USS* Polaris, *the First US Expedition to the North Pole*. New York: New American Library, 2001. Print. 171.

11. Ibid. 222.

12. Alec Wilkinson. *The Ice Balloon: S. A. Andree and the Heroic Age of Arctic Exploration*. New York: Knopf, 2011. Print. 15–16.

13. Bruce Henderson. "Cook Vs. Peary." *Smithsonian* 40.1 (2009): 58–69. *Academic Search Premier*. Web. 28 Apr. 2013.

14. Marilyn J. Landis. *Antarctica: Exploring the Extreme—Four Hundred Years of Adventure*. Chicago: Chicago Review, 2001. Print. 170–171.

15. "Thickness of the Antarctic Ice Cap." *The Physics Factbook*. Hypertextbook, 2000. Web. 28 Aug. 2013.

16. "Which Pole is Colder?" *Climate Kids*. NASA, n.d. Web. 28 Aug. 2013.

17. Bruce Henderson. *Fatal North: Adventure and Survival Aboard USS* Polaris, *the First US Expedition to the North Pole*. New York: New American Library, 2001. Print. 23.

CHAPTER 2. QUESTS FOR A NORTHWEST PASSAGE

1. David Mountfield. "A History of Polar Exploration." London: Hamlyn, 1974. Print. 19.

2. Charles Emmerson. *The Future History of the Arctic*. New York: Public Affairs, 2010. 6.

3. Evan Hadingham. "The Secrets of Viking Ships." *Nova*. PBS, 9 May 2000. Web. 24 May 2013.

4. Priit J. Vesilind. "In Search of Vikings." *National Geographic*. National Geographic, May 2000. Web. 22 May 2013.

5. Mick Conefrey and Tim Jordan. *Icemen*. New York: TV Books, 1998. Print. 26.

6. Ibid. 30.

7. Ibid. 32.

8. Ibid.

9. Ibid. 75.

10. Ibid. 76.

CHAPTER 3. IN SEARCH OF A SOUTHERN CONTINENT

1. Joan Boothe. *The Storied Ice: Exploration, Discovery, and Adventure in Antarctica's Peninsula Region*. Berkeley, CA: Regent Press, 2011. Print. 22.

2. Ibid. 30–31.

3. David McGonigal and Lynn Woodworth. *The Complete Encyclopedia: Antarctica and the Arctic*. Willowdale, Ontario: Firefly Books, 2001. Print. 409.

4. Ibid. 417.

5. Ibid. 418.

6. Thomas Arnold. *The American Practical Lunarian and Seaman's Guide*. Philadelphia: Robert Desilver, 1822. *Google Book Search*. Web. 28 Aug. 2013.

7. Marilyn J. Landis. *Antarctica: Exploring the Extreme—Four Hundred Years of Adventure*. Chicago: Chicago Review, 2001. Print. 196.

8. "Physical Facts about Antarctica." *Cold Science*. USA Today, 2008. Web. 28 Aug. 2013.

CHAPTER 4. HEROIC JOURNEYS TO THE NORTH

1. Bruce Henderson. "Cook vs. Peary." *Smithsonian* 40.1 (2009): 58–69. *Academic Search Premier*. Web. 28 Apr. 2013.

2. Ibid.

3. Ibid.

4. Ibid.

5. Mick Conefrey and Tim Jordan. *Icemen*. New York: TV Books, 1998. Print. 51.

6. Bruce Henderson. "Cook vs. Peary." *Smithsonian* 40.1 (2009): 58–69. *Academic Search Premier*. Web. 28 Apr. 2013.

7. Ibid.

8. Ibid.

9. Mick Conefrey and Tim Jordan. *Icemen*. New York: TV Books, 1998. Print. 65.

10. D. D. Jackson. "Lincoln Ellsworth, The Forgotten Hero of Polar Exploration." *Smithsonian* 21.7 (1990): 171. *Academic Search Premier*. Web. 28 Apr. 2013.

11. Mick Conefrey and Tim Jordan. *Icemen*. New York: TV Books, 1998. Print. 91.

12. D. D. Jackson. "Lincoln Ellsworth, The Forgotten Hero of Polar Exploration." *Smithsonian* 21.7 (1990): 171. *Academic Search Premier*. Web. 28 Apr. 2013.

13. Mick Conefrey and Tim Jordan. *Icemen*. New York: TV Books, 1998. Print. 92–93.

14. Ibid. 94.

SOURCE NOTES CONTINUED

15. "The Norge Flight Across the Arctic (1926)." *The Fram Museum*. The Fram Museum, n.d. Web. 4 June 2013.

16. Mick Conefrey and Tim Jordan. *Icemen*. New York: TV Books, 1998. Print. 100.

CHAPTER 5. THE RACE TO TERRA INCOGNITA

1. Marilyn J. Landis. *Antarctica: Exploring the Extreme—Four Hundred Years of Adventure*. Chicago: Chicago Review, 2001. Print. 127.

2. Ibid. 237–239.

3. Ibid. 241.

4. Ibid. 151.

5. Ross D. E. MacPhee. *Race to the End: Amundsen, Scott, and the Attainment of the South Pole*. New York: Sterling, 2010. Print. 60.

6. Lynne Cox. *South with the Sun: Roald Amundsen, His Polar Explorations, and the Quest for Discovery*. New York: Knopf, 2011. Print. 31.

7. Ross D. E. MacPhee. *Race to the End: Amundsen, Scott, and the Attainment of the South Pole*. New York: Sterling Innovation, 2010. Print. 85.

8. Marilyn J. Landis. *Antarctica: Exploring the Extreme—Four Hundred Years of Adventure*. Chicago: Chicago Review, 2001. Print. 158.

9. Ibid. 159.

10. Marilyn J. Landis. *Antarctica: Exploring the Extreme—Four Hundred Years of Adventure*. Chicago: Chicago Review, 2001. Print. 160.

11. Ross D. E. MacPhee. *Race to the End: Amundsen, Scott, and the Attainment of the South Pole*. New York: Sterling, 2010. Print. 162.

12. Ibid.

13. Ibid. 177.

14. Ibid. 180.

15. Ibid. 193.

CHAPTER 6. EXPLORING BY AIR AND BY SEA IN THE ARCTIC

1. Charles Emmerson. *The Future History of the Arctic*. New York: Public Affairs, 2010. Print. 82.

2. Mick Conefrey and Tim Jordan. *Icemen*. New York: TV Books, 1998. Print. 147.

3. Ibid. 150.

4. Ibid. 153.

5. Andrew Revkin. "On Top of the World." *New York Times*. New York Times, 13 May 2003. Web. 8 June 2013.

CHAPTER 7. CONFLICT AND COMPROMISE IN ANTARCTICA

1. Joan Boothe. *The Storied Ice: Exploration, Discovery, and Adventure in Antarctica's Peninsula Region*. Berkeley, CA: Regent, 2011. Print. 213–217.

2. Ibid. 221–223.

3. Marilyn J. Landis. *Antarctica: Exploring the Extreme—Four Hundred Years of Adventure*. Chicago: Chicago Review, 2001. Print. 176.

4. Joan Boothe. *The Storied Ice: Exploration, Discovery, and Adventure in Antarctica's Peninsula Region*. Berkeley, CA: Regent, 2011. Print. 223.

5. Ibid. 227–230.

6. David McGonigal and Lynn Woodworth. *The Complete Encyclopedia: Antarctica and the Arctic*. Willowdale, Ontario: Firefly, 2001. Print. 495.

7. Ibid. 501.

8. Joan Boothe. *The Storied Ice: Exploration, Discovery, and Adventure in Antarctica's Peninsula Region*. Berkeley, CA: Regent, 2011. Print. 275.

9. Ibid.

10. Ibid. 270–271.

11. Ellyn Hammet. "A Warmer Climate for Women in Antarctica." *Origins Antarctica*. National Science Foundation, n.d. Web. 9 June 2013.

12. Marilyn J. Landis. *Antarctica: Exploring the Extreme—Four Hundred Years of Adventure*. Chicago: Chicago Review, 2001. Print. 185.

13. Joan Boothe. *The Storied Ice: Exploration, Discovery, and Adventure in Antarctica's Peninsula Region*. Berkeley, CA: Regent, 2011. Print. 276.

CHAPTER 8. THE FUTURE OF POLAR EXPLORATION

1. Mick Conefrey and Tim Jordan. *Icemen*. New York: TV Books, 1998. Print. 177.

2. Ibid. 179.

3. "New Report on the State of Polar Regions." *Science Daily*. Science Daily, 3 Apr. 2012. Web. 28 Aug. 2013.

4. Nick Perry and Rod McGuirk. "Antarctic Ice Samples: What Do They Say about Global Warming?" *Christian Science Monitor*. Christian Science Monitor, 6 Apr. 2013. Web. 9 June 2013.

5. Jon Bowermaster. "Global Warming Changing Inuit Lands, Lives, Arctic Expedition Shows." *National Geographic News*. National Geographic, 15 May 2007. Web. 28 Aug. 2013.

6. David Unger. "China Looks North for Oil, Gas and Fish." *Christian Science Monitor*. Christian Science Monitor, 15 May 2013. Web. 9 June 2013.

7. "The Expedition." *The Coldest Journey*. The Coldest Journey.org, 2013. Web. 9 June 2013.

8. Alexander Kumar. "The Coldest Journey on Earth." *New York Times*. New York Times, 21 Sept. 2012. Web. 9 June 2013.

INDEX

ABOUT THE AUTHOR

Judy Dodge Cummings is a writer and history teacher from Wisconsin. She is the author of *Civil War* and several other books. Although she has traveled extensively on five of the seven continents, she has not yet been to either the North or South Pole.